Our world is changing—quickly . . . transforming itself into a brave new age that will require new values, technologies, and lifestyles. In this highly astute assessment of the years to come, controversial futurist FM-2030 shows you which attitudes and trends will survive—and which will go the way of the dinosaurs. You'll discover how sweeping social, economic, medical, political, and technological changes will affect the way people live, love, work, and play . . . and how some people, the "transhumans," will make a smooth transition into this time—while others will be left behind. Most important, you'll learn how the person you are today can make the most of the wonders of tomorrow.

"FM is one of the first thinkers in history to live, teach, plan, and campaign for a future for mankind as a universal species. He has suggested in bold controversial terms an utterly new way of life."
—*The Futurist* **on FM's previous book,** *Up-Wingers*

"A prophet of Boom. . . . He maintains 'we are at the beginning of an age of limitless abundance . . . and an age of immortality.' "
—*New York Times*

"An engaging visionary and a lover of humankind . . . FM has the transcendental presence of a master."
—*New Age* **magazine**

About the Author

"I AM A 21ST-CENTURY PERSON WHO WAS ACCIDENTALLY LAUNCHED IN THE 20TH. I HAVE A DEEP NOSTALGIA FOR THE FUTURE." —FM-2030

Born with a conventional name, FM-2030 (twenty-thirty) changed both his first and last names to reflect his beliefs and confidence in the future. As he explains, "conventional names define a person's past: ancestry, ethnicity, nationality, religion. Long ago I outgrew such territorialities. I am not who I was ten years ago and certainly not who I will be in twenty years. I would rather be defined by my future—my hopes and dreams. The name 2030 reflects my conviction that the years around 2030 will be a magical time. The solar system will be alive with people linking in and out of planets and moons and orbital communities. In 2030 we will be ageless and everyone will have an excellent chance to live forever. 2030 is a dream and a goal."

FM-2030 is the author of several pioneering books on the future, including *Optimism One, Up-Wingers,* and *Telespheres.* A renowned philosopher, formerly with the United Nations, he is currently a consultant to industry, government, film and TV productions, and the Space Agency. He is a dreamer, a visionary, a social critic, a futurist with "a hailstorm of ideas." (*Washington Post*)

ARE YOU A TRANSHUMAN?

Monitoring and Stimulating
Your Personal Rate of Growth
In a Rapidly Changing World

by
FM-2030

WARNER BOOKS

A Warner Communications Company

Warner Books, Inc., 666 Fifth Avenue, New York, NY 10103

A Warner Communications Company

Printed in the United States of America
First Printing: January 1989
10 9 8 7 6 5 4 3 2

Library of Congress Cataloging-in-Publication Data

FM-2030.
 Are you a transhuman?
 1. Social perception. 2. Self-evaluation. I. Title.
BF323.S63F56 1989 158'.1 88-20436
ISBN 0-446-38806-8

Dedications and Acknowledgments

This book is dedicated to fellow transhumans everywhere.

I wish to express particular appreciation to the following:

My mother and father who gave me one of the loveliest gifts parents can offer their children—the opportunity to grow up all over the planet.

Farida and Fay—for their humanity.

Flora—friend and companion and longtime supporter of Up-Wing objectives.

Sylvana—Terrine—Emiliano—John H.—Nancie (NC)—for their companionship and collaboration.

Fellow activists in the Immortality and Space programs.

The people at our futurist seminars—particularly at the New School for Social Research in New York and at UCLA (Extension). Their curiosity and enthusiasm has made the exploration of the future all the more stimulating.

Dean Allen Austill—Lester Singer—Wally—who in the 1960s gave me a launching pad for my ideas at the New School at a time when the study of the future had not yet crystallized into a discipline.

Emilie Jacobson—my literary representative at Curtis Brown—for her support and confidence.

My editors at various publishing houses through the years. Particularly Harry Braverman at Grove Press. Merril Polack at W. W. Norton. Pat O'Connor at Fawcett. Jamie Raab at Warner Books. For their receptivity to new ideas.

Contents

Foreword

The central purpose of this interactive book is to help you monitor and improve your rate of personal growth (RPG) in a rapidly changing world. To this end—the book is comprised of twenty-five self-tests—each of which has been designed to explore a different area of development and to answer such vital questions as:

How updated are you in an age when information—values—lifestyles—technology—depreciate quickly?

How on track are you in an age of discontinuity when the guideposts change all the time and it is therefore easy to lose one's bearings?

How well does your adaptability rate adjust at a time of swift recontextings?

How clear are you about your professional and investment directions at a time when entire professions and technologies phase out and new ones phase in?

How stuck are you in the high-stress–low-yield industrial world at a time when you can shift to the low-stress–high-yield postindustrial stage?

These self-tests are intended as a gyroscope—an aligner—an accelerator. They offer a unique means of learning more about yourself and what the future promises for all of us.

The title of this book *Are You a Transhuman?* anticipates massive changes ahead. Most of the self-tests contained here focus on immediate everyday changes in our lives. However—as I explain in the final chapter—we are at the beginning of the age of transhumans (a stage beyond the human). Persistent advances in many areas of life are forging fundamental transformations in the human condition. These changes will grow all too evident in the coming years. The title serves as a reminder of the Larger Picture that is steadily crystallizing all around us.

Scoring Procedure

Go over each monitor (question sheet) and give your answer to each question.

Give answers that most closely reflect your positions. Don't skip any questions.

Then turn to the answer sheet that follows each monitor and score your answers. The numbers in parentheses indicate the points you give yourself for each answer. No number indicates zero value.

At the end of the self-tests add up your scores for all twenty-five monitors. The total points will give you an *approximate* measure of your rate of personal growth (RPG). The implications of your final score will be discussed in the conclusion of the book.

On most questions there are no right or wrong answers.

The questions assume the direction and the pace at which I see us progressing—particularly here in North America.

These self-tests are not conclusive but suggestive.

The monitors in this book are based on my work in the field of forecasting and long-range planning since the early 1960s. I have used variations of these self-tests in my seminars at the New School for Social Research—UCLA (Extension)—and at countless seminars and workshops conducted for professional groups—corporations—government agencies—scientific organizations.

How Updated Is Your Vocabulary?

Below are two lists of commonly used terms. Working your way down the page, check the term from either column A or column B that is closer to what you would use.

Column A	Column B
1 ____ Boyfriend–girlfriend	____ Friend–lover
2 ____ Bachelor	____ Single
3 ____ Unsuccessful marriage	____ Dissolved marriage
4 ____ Illegitimate child	____ Child
5 ____ Broken home	____ Single-parent home
6 ____ Promiscuous	____ Fluid—open—liberated
7 ____ Test-tube baby	____ In vitro fertilized baby— high-tech baby
8 ____ Homosexual	____ Gay
9 ____ Sex object	____ Lover
10 ____ Pornography	____ Erotica
11 ____ Relationship	____ Romance—friendship— linkup
12 ____ Courtesy title: Mr.— Mrs.—Miss—Ms.	____ No courtesy titles. Only names.
13 ____ Doctor Jones (physician)	____ Sam or Sam Jones

14 ____ Secretary   ____ Assistant—associate

15 ____ Leader   ____ Catalyst—facilitator

16 ____ Masses   ____ People

17 ____ Foreigner—alien   ____ Visitor (from abroad)

18 ____ Spiritual   ____ Religious—devout

19 ____ Holy places—holy land   ____ Religious places

20 ____ God bless   ____ Good-bye or May the force be with you!

21 ____ God willing   ____ Let's go for it.

22 ____ Artificial insemination ____ Insemination (or asexual insemination)

23 ____ Artificial organs   ____ Prostheses—replacement parts

24 ____ Artificial intelligence ____ Ultraintelligent machines

25 ____ Far East   ____ East Asia

26 ____ Middle or Near East   ____ West Asia

27 ____ Far West (in the U.S.)   ____ Western states

28 ____ Free World   ____ Western world

29 ____ Third World   ____ Developing regions

30 ____ Man   ____ Humankind

Answer sheet: MONITOR 1

	Column A		Column B	
1	_____	(0 points	_____	(2 points
2	_____	for each item	_____	for each item
3	_____	in column A)	_____	in column B)
4	_____		_____	
5	_____		_____	
6	_____		_____	
7	_____		_____	
8	_____		_____	
9	_____		_____	
10	_____		_____	
11	_____		_____	
12	_____		_____	
13	_____		_____	
14	_____		_____	
15	_____		_____	
16	_____		_____	
17	_____		_____	
18	_____		_____	
19	_____		_____	
20	_____		_____	
21	_____		_____	
22	_____		_____	
23	_____		_____	
24	_____		_____	
25	_____		_____	
26	_____		_____	
27	_____		_____	
28	_____		_____	
29	_____		_____	
30	_____		_____	

Total: _____   _____

How updated is your vocabulary?

Our changing values and technology are often reflected in our everyday speech.

You can tell much about people's orientations by their vocabulary. People who hold on to old attitudes and hardware as a rule use outdated terminologies. People who have shifted to new time zones have updated vocabularies. This is illustrated by the examples that follow.

Boyfriend/girlfriend. It is laughable hearing adults thirty and forty and fifty years old refer to their lovers as "girlfriends" and "boyfriends." No wonder so many people behave like adolescents in their romances.

"I am going away with my boyfriend this weekend"—a forty-two-year-old woman says.

" 'Boyfriend'? What is he—a twelve-year-old?"

What then does one call a person with whom one makes love?

A "friend." A "lover."

Bachelor. This is a reactive term from the days when married life was the norm. If you were not married you were a "bachelor."

Other anachronistic terms: maiden—spinster—old maid.

"Single" is a modern term signifying a new way of life for millions of people.

Unsuccessful marriage. Any marriage that lasts for even a few hours is successful. In our times the duration of a linkup does not determine its success or failure.

People who go about stigmatizing their dissolved marriages as "failures" flog themselves with outdated ethics.

Illegitimate child. There is nothing "illegitimate" about a child born to people who are pioneering new options for parenthood.

Broken home. This too is a pejorative term from the days when marriage was considered permanent. Adults and children paid a heavy price for forced constancy. The only "broken homes" are those where parents fight all the time yet hold on to each other at all cost. It is the children particularly who suffer in this venomous atmosphere.

Parents who decouple create not broken homes but "multiple homes" for their children. Such fluid arrangements are not alien to today's children.

Promiscuous. This is a hangover term from unliberated times when making love with anyone other than your spouse or permanent sexual partner was considered promiscuous. By these standards *everyone* in a modern society is promiscuous.
The fact is that people today are not promiscuous. They are fluid.

Test-tube baby. There is nothing "test-tube" about the tens of thousands of babies born every year through new procreation techniques. "High-tech baby" is certainly more appropriate.

Gay. This is the term that seems to be preferred by the homosexual community.

Sex object. This term carries an implied disapproval. But in our times when millions of people are voluntarily not reproducing—it is perfectly understandable to want people just for sex—as lovers (sex objects).

Pornography. Pornography has long had sleazy and prurient connotations. The fact is that what was considered lewd and filthy twenty years ago is now accepted as normal.
Erotica (pornography) has pervaded all areas of modern life: neighborhood movie theaters—cable TV—prime-time TV "soaps"—videocassettes—magazines—newspapers—books.
The norms are changing. Much of what is considered "dirty" or obscene today will be perfectly acceptable in a few years.

Relationship. In America this word was bandied about all through the 1940s—'50s—'60s—'70s. Everyone talked about their "relationships." "Making the relationship work." "Committing yourself to a relationship." "Working with your analyst on the relationship."
In its time the word "relationship" reflected a wholesome new attitude—a departure from the restrictive Victorian morality of earlier times.
But the term "relationship" does not fit into the rhythm and spirit of our times. Relationships are too slow and territorial for our change-over decades.

We need new terms. Perhaps "linkup" or "connection." Even "romance" or "friendship."

"Linkup" is my favorite. It captures the mood and the pace of the 1980s and the 1990s.

A linkup is open and uncomplicated. A linkup may last one night or one month or one year or ten years or one hundred years. It may be exclusive for a while. But it is often nonexclusive. It is certainly fluid.

Courtesy titles: Mr.—Mrs.—Miss—Ms. Do you address people as Excellency or Eminence or Highness? Not long ago such courtesy titles were commonplace. (In hierarchical societies they still are.) People felt slighted if not addressed with the appropriate formalities.

Egalitarian societies such as the United States have largely done away with such pomposities. "Mr." and "Mrs." are holdovers from hierarchical times. "Ms." is no less of an affectation.

Why do we need any titles at all? Why not address people by their names? This certainly moves us toward greater equality.

Addressing people by their names is an insult only to people who do not like their names.

Doctor Jones (when addressing a physician). Do you go around addressing people by their professional affiliations? Engineer Nelson. Attorney Schnall. Artist Voltolini.

Why then address your physician as "doctor"?

Titles only reinforce distances among us.

No wonder many people are in awe of physicians. Such people expect too much of their doctors. If there is a slipup—a very human tendency—the awe quickly degenerates into massive disappointment and anger.

Unfortunately too many physicians encourage this distance between themselves and their patients. They end up paying a heavy price these days for insisting on playing a dominant role.

Secretary. People who refer to their office associates as secretaries are flexing bureaucratic muscles. They are showing off.

People who refer to themselves as secretaries lack professional self-esteem.

The fact is that in the age of smart machines and automated offices and work-from-anywhere occupations—the secretary is phasing out.

Leader. "Leader" and "leadership" are holdovers from primitive times. Leadership by its very nature is inherently authoritarian. Leadership and followship automatically mean the unequal distribution of power and influence. A society or an organization that emphasizes leadership is not modern or democratic.

In the postindustrial world of decentralization and shared decision making "leader" is just as outdated as "Master" and "Lord" and "head of household."

(More on this in monitors 8: Power Oriented and 20: Ideology.)

Masses. Personal global telecommunication and global mobility are eroding mass conformity. There are no masses in postindustrial societies.

Foreigner. In our age of cross-planetary dialogue and global migrations the term "foreigner" sounds forced and anachronistic.

People who still emphasize terms such as "foreigner" and "alien" tend to view the world as rigidly compartmentalized into us and them.

This planet belongs to all of us. There are no foreigners or aliens any longer.

Spiritual. This word is often a camouflage.

People who are embarrassed to be called religious refer to themselves as spiritual. The fact is that the spiritual—no matter how nimbly they tap dance around it—are religious. They just don't want to admit it. Scratch the surface a little and you will find a religious person hiding inside.

The term "spiritual" is also an affectation. The spiritual tend to be self-righteous. But they have nothing to be self-righteous about.

People who are enlightened and humanistic do not go around calling themselves spiritual. They *live* their ethics. Their actions speak for themselves.

(More on this in Monitor 23: Your Level of Humanity.)

Holy: holy land—holy books—holy men. The idea of holiness is a central facet of the fairy tales and superstitions nurtured during humanity's long childhood. The term "holy" carries a value judgment. Why not call "a holy place" what it really is—a religious place.

God willing and god bless. Appeals to gods are commonplace among people who do not manage their own lives but who always "look up" to higher forces—parents and gurus and leaders and gods—to take care of them.

Artificial. This is a favorite term of purists and fundamentalists. The fact is that *anything* that unfolds in this world is part of this nature and cannot be artificial.

There are no artificial foods—no artificial organs—no artificial intelligence. There is no artificial anything.

Prosthetic replacement parts made of silicone and Dacron and oxygen are just as natural as organic parts made of calcium and proteins and iron.

What is so artificial about an intelligent brain that can make billions of computations a second?

This emphasis on distinctions between the "natural" and the "artificial" is itself artificial. It reinforces people's resistance to making changes in themselves and in their environments—changes that are essential if we are to evolve to more sophisticated beings.

Far East. Where is the Far East far from? If you live in China or Japan or Korea do you live in the "Far" East? Is China "far" to the one billion Chinese?

How would you like people on other continents referring to your regions as Far United States and Far West and Far Europe?

The fact is that there is no Far East or Middle East or Near East. These are all designations from the colonial period—eighteenth and nineteenth centuries—when European powers were dominant in the world. Everything was measured in relation to Europe. The "Near East" was near Europe. The "Far East" was far from Europe.

Far West (in the U.S.). This is as anachronistic as the term "back East." The people in Oregon do not think of themselves as living far away.

Free World. People who use such propagandist terms are themselves not free.

Third World. This does not strike me as a useful term. It tends to polarize the world into adversarial camps of have-nations and have-not nations.

The fact is that there is poverty and certainly backwardness everywhere in the world—even in the more prosperous nations. The poor and the backward in Alabama and in Sicily do not live in the "Third World" but they too urgently need attention.

Then too there are now enclaves of wealth and advanced technology in most "Third World" countries.

There must be better ways of focussing attention on the poor and the backward of the world.

Man. This word—when used to denote humankind—is grating to modern enlightened sensibilities.

How Telespheral-age (Postindustrial) Are You?

1– How significant are distinctions between the industrial age and the postindustrial?

_____Profound
_____Moderate
_____Negligible

2– How high-tech is your home? For example do you deploy:

A– Smart telephones (memory — automatic dial — teleconference — call forwarding)
B– Answering machine
C– Global radio (shortwave)
D– Audio recorder
E– Video recorder
F– VCR
G– Disc player
H– Modem (computer/telephone hookup)
I– Videotex and teletext access
J– Picturephone
K– Satellite dish
L– Interactive TV
M– Large-screen TV

A _____Yes _____No
B _____Yes _____No
C _____Yes _____No
D _____Yes _____No
E _____Yes _____No
F _____Yes _____No
G _____Yes _____No
H _____Yes _____No
I _____Yes _____No
K _____Yes _____No
L _____Yes _____No
M _____Yes _____No

3– How automated is your work environment?

A– Word-processing
B– Printer
C– Telex
D– Local area networks (group of computers sharing work)
E– Facsimile
F– Computerized organizer
G– Videoconferencing
H– Audio/video recording
I– Decision-assist
J– Expert systems
K– Ultraintelligent (AI) capabilities
L– Telemail (electronic mail)

A _____Yes _____No
B _____Yes _____No
C _____Yes _____No
D _____Yes _____No
E _____Yes _____No
F _____Yes _____No
G _____Yes _____No
H _____Yes _____No
I _____Yes _____No
J _____Yes _____No
K _____Yes _____No
L _____Yes _____No

4– Where do you do your work?
    A– Office: daily commuting?   ————
    B– Telecommuting: no commuting.
         Work at plugged-in home?   ————
    C– Flex work environment: home and
         office and satellite office and car and
         resort?   ————

5– How much of your personal business do you transact via telebanking (electronic home banking)? For example electronic bill payments.

————Extensive
————Some
————None

6– How much of your information needs do you access via: television seminars —telelectures—telephone or computer links to data banks—teletext?

————Extensive
————Some
————None

7– How much teleshopping do you do (electronic home shopping via cable TV or telecatalog)?

————Extensive
————Some
————None

8– How plugged in are you to telemedicine: telemonitoring—telediagnosis— teletherapy—telemed info banks?

————Extensive
————Some
————None

9– How teleconnected are you *personally?*
Do you carry:

		Yes	No	Yes	No
A– Portable telephone	**E**– Car telephone	——	——	——	——
B– Wrist or pocket TV	**F**– Portable answering machine				
C– Pocket recorder	**G**– Headphone				
D– Portable computer					

Answer sheet: MONITOR 2

1   ____Profound (2)   ____Moderate (1)

                                ____Negligible

2

		Yes	No	Yes	No
A	G	____(2)	____	____(2)	____
	H			____(2)	____
B	I	____(2)	____	____(2)	____
C		____(2)	____		
D	J	____(2)	____	____(2)	____
E	K	____(2)	____	____(2)	____
F	L	____(2)	____	____(2)	____
	M			____(2)	____

3

		Yes	No	Yes	No
A	G	____(2)	____	____(2)	____
B	H	____(2)	____	____(2)	____
C	I	____(2)	____	____(2)	____
D	J	____(2)	____	____(2)	____
	K			____(2)	____
E		____(2)	____		
F	L	____(2)	____	____(2)	____

4

A   ____

B   ____(1)

C   ____(2)

5   ____Extensive (2)

          ____Some (1)

          ____None

6   ____Extensive (2)

          ____Some (1)

          ____None

7   ____Extensive (2)
                     ____Some (1)
                     ____None

8   ____Extensive (2)
                     ____Some (1)
                     ____None

9   Yes   No   Yes   No
  A   E   ____(2)   ____   ____(2)   ____
  B   F   ____(2)   ____   ____(2)   ____
  C   G   ____(2)   ____   ____(2)   ____
  D   ____(2)   ____

Total: _____

Distinctions between the industrial age and the postindustrial.

We can already see the differences between the industrial age and the new age. The distinctions are basic and profound.

The differences between industrialism and the next stage are primarily differences in the way we organize and deploy energy and information.

(I call the postindustrial world the *tele*spheral age precisely because telecommunication more than ever will play a central pivotal role.)

The new telecom is already playing havoc with the way we have traditionally organized our time and space.

In this emerging electronic environment far and near—small and large—slow and fast—powerful and powerless—right and left are beginning to lose meaning.

For example in the telespheral environment you do not travel to access services. Services come to you—wherever *you* are.

The stage beyond school education is teleducation.

The stage beyond the hospital is telemedicine.

This is a new world of telegenesis—telenetwork—telebanking—

teleshopping—telecommuting—teleconferencing—teledemocracy—etc.

In the industrial world people are rushed to a hospital *after* they have succumbed to an illness. In the postindustrial environment you are hooked up to medical services—the protective preventive care is within you—wherever you are. In case of an imminent malfunction telemed automatically alerts you—often before you yourself are aware of a malfunction.

Such protective telemedical support is already provided to many homebound elderly people via Lifeline and to ambulatory cardiac patients via remote monitoring. In the coming years more and more *healthy* people will have such continuous protection.

Then too videotex services in some cities of North America and Western Europe have introduced electronic home banking—electronic shopping—teleducation (via two-way TV seminars)—electronic information retrieval (telelibrary)—instant voting and polling (teledemocracy).

In the telespheral world everything is decentralized—despecialized—demonopolized—debureaucratized—globalized.

Here is a shorthand breakdown of *some* of the distinctions between the industrial age and the telespheral:

Industrial age	Telespheral age
One-way broadcast communication	Two-way interactive telecom
Labor-intensive mechanical technology	Technology-intensive self-operating systems
Finite monopolizable sources of energy	Limitless cheap nonmonopolizable energy
Economics based on heavy industry	Economics based on information and services
Authoritarian/hereditarian family units	Fluid reciprocal networks
Values based on hardship—puritanism—scarcity	Values based on pleasure—leisure—abundance
Short life expectancies 50 or 60 years	Life spans beyond 120
Limited growth within this planet	Limitless growth across the solar system and beyond

The above telespheral tracks do not run parallel to one another. They interconnect and reinforce one another organizing life in fundamentally new ways.

We are at the very beginning of the postindustrial age. We do not know *exactly* how things will coalesce. But we do know that the ethical—social—economic—political—international transformations will be profound.

Some implications of the teleconnected environment.

Telecommunication is as indispensable to the telespheral world as the plowshare was in the agrarian period and the smokestack or the automobile in the industrial.

The freeways and byways of the new age are the electronic and photonic circuits that connect all areas of life.

The more telecom systems you deploy the more telespheral (electronic) your environment. The fewer telecom the more industrial age your world.

Technology and social values are interconnected. It is not possible to advance to new enlightened values and lifestyles (for example leisure and fluidity) if you still hold on to old technology.

As I will attempt to show in the coming pages the shift to a new age is more than an upgrade of hardware. It is also a rescripting of ethics and social values.

Then too it is no longer possible to be productive and effective in today's world without the paraphernalia of high-tech.

If you live and work in a low-tech environment you are at a disadvantage because the world around you is increasingly high-tech.

In the telespheral world the home—work environment—recreation decenters—transportation vehicles are all teleconnected. In fact as we advance into this new age play and work and transportation all merge.

How plugged in are you personally?

It is no longer enough to live and play and work in teleconnected environments. You yourself need to be hooked-up—wherever you are.

In our age of high mobility and decentralized communities we need to be in reach at all times and in all places.

At one time the idea of a telephone or a two-way computer linking the home with the outside world was considered futuristic. The day will soon come when not just every home—but every individual—will carry in and on the body small transceivers.

Portable telephones—TVs—radios—computers—answering systems—receptor wristwatches are already available. Portable telephones are particularly valuable. They offer the following obvious advantages:

• You are able to connect from wherever you are. Reach out and be reached. You are never in a communication blackout.

• You are never alone. If you want privacy simply disconnect your mobile system.

• You are able to teleconference—telebank—teleshop—telemarket —telelearn—telemail—or access other services from wherever you are. (This automatically opens up an abundance of leisure time.)

• You have quick direct access to emergency services anytime any-where. (Every day people die because they cannot call out for help or help arrives too late.)

• You are also able to instantly seek help for others in distress.

Soon no telespheral-age person will venture anywhere without some onbody two-way hookup. We are entering the age of the telehuman.

Won't such a technology-intensive environment leave many people behind because they will not be skilled at using the new hardware?

One of the magical qualities of high tech is that the more sophisticated it grows the easier it is to operate.

Want to use a smart telephone? Simply *tell* your friendly machine who you want to call or what service you need to access and it will do the rest.

Want to telebank? Simply connect with your bank—even cross-planet—log in your code number and the service will pay all your bills or transfer funds.

Soon you will dialogue with your computer in everyday (natural)

language and your smart little companion will do everything for you—
short of massaging and fondling you.

In the age of print large numbers of people everywhere were not able
to acquire the difficult skills of reading and writing and were therefore
perpetually at a disadvantage.

In the electronic world no one will be left behind because everyone
can activate a TV or use a telephone or dialogue with a smart machine.

The more intelligent and complex a machine the easier it is to use.

If you do your work and shopping and learning and everything else from your home or wherever won't that lead to isolation?

When television sets began to proliferate in the late 1940s and the 1950s
everyone worried: "If one day every home has a TV set and everyone
stays in—won't that isolate people?"

Today everyone has a TV set. Yet more people eat in restaurants—
sit in cafes—dance at discos—go to the movies and stroll in the streets
than ever.

The new electronic environment—once we adjust to it—will actually
reduce isolation and loneliness.

By deploying the new electronic services you accomplish more in
less time and with less effort and therefore create more *free* time to do
as you wish.

I have a friend in Santa Monica, California, who lives near the ocean.
He does most of his work at home via telephone and computer and
telex. He works for a few hours every day and by two o'clock in the
afternoon he closes up "shop" and links up with a friend or friends for
a walk on the beach or lunch at an oceanside restaurant.

Then too the new way of doing work and accessing services from
wherever you are does not preclude meeting in person with colleagues
and clients. You now have the latitude to choose when and where to
rendezvous.

What does efficiency mean in the telespheral age?

In the agrarian world the efficient person rode a horse or a donkey to
the fields to farm and to the market to obtain provisions.

In the industrial age the efficient person commutes to work and school and shopping malls.

In the telespheral age the efficient use of time means connecting from wherever *you* are.

Commuting to work every day is industrial age. An office is an anachronism. There is no such thing as a "modern office."

You rush to work every day—traveling an hour or longer—fighting traffic—only to end up sitting in an office making connections via telephone or computer or videoconference. Why not do all this from home or beach or wherever you are?

To be efficient in our times means using high tech in a high-tech manner. People who squander hours every day commuting to a "modern" automated office make low-tech use of high tech. This is like transporting your computer to a data bank each time you wish to access information.

To be efficient in our times means never standing in line at a bank but telebanking from wherever you are.

To be efficient in our times means never having to drive across the city to a library to do research but connecting with information outlets from wherever you are.

To be efficient in our times means . . .

Many people in industrial-age societies are hard pressed because they do not make intelligent use of their time—resources—new technology.

The speed in the transmission of information and services has accelerated yet many people are still bogged down in an industrial-age pace of doing things.

Efficiency in our new age entails extensive and intelligent use of telecommunication. To be efficient is to be telefficient.

How Information Rich Are You?

1–How many global newspapers do you read every day?
For example: *New York Times— Washington Post—Los Angeles Times—Wall Street Journal—Le Monde—International Herald Tribune*—etc.

___2 or more
___1
___None

2–How many general interest news magazines do you read every week?
For example: *Time—Newsweek— U.S. News & World Report—The Nation—Atlantic—Harper's*—etc.

___2 or more
___1
___None

3–How many general interest science magazines a month?
Scientific American—Science News —Popular Science—Discover— Omni—Science—Psychology Today—etc.

___3 or more
___1 or 2
___None

4–How many *specialized* publications do you read every week?
Journals of medicine—astronomy —computers—economics—etc.

___2 or more
___1
___None

5–How many books do you read every year?

___Over 10   ___Under 10

6–How many hours in an average day do you watch television?

___Over 1 hr ___Under 1 hr

7–How many films do you see every week?

___2 or more   ___Under 2

8–How often do you listen to radio news and interviews?

____Over 1 hr daily
____Under 1 hr daily

9–How many audio/video cassettes or discs or telemagazines do you listen to every week?

____Over 10   ____Under 10

10–How often do you use a computer to access information-retrieval services (data banks—teletext—electronic bulletin boards—etc.)?

____Several times a week
____Rarely or never

11–How many seminars do you attend every year?

____Over 5   ____Under 5

12–How many conferences (or conventions) do you attend every year?

____Over 5   ____Under 5

13–How often do you travel out of your city every year?
    A–How often out of the country every year?

____Over 10 trips __Under 10

____Over 3 trips ____Under 3

14–How much of your knowledge base is specialized (for example within a specific profession or area of interest)?
    A–When you read a magazine or newspaper do you only focus on your area of interest (politics or arts or sciences or sports or specific nation)?

____Much   ____Some

____Always   ____Sometimes
       ____Never

15–How well do you speak and understand and read English?

____Very well ____Quite well
       ____Not well

16–How well do you understand the dynamics of the new information age? For example:

   A–Who controls information in our electronic age?

      ____Gov't   ____Media barons
      ____Powerful interests
      ____No one in particular

   B–How costly is it to be well-informed?

      ____Costly   ____Cheap

   C–Do you ever suffer from information overload?

      ____Often   ____Sometimes
      ____Never

Answer sheet: MONITOR 3

1 ____2 or more (2)   ____1 (1)   ____None

2 ____2 or more (2)   ____1 (1)   ____None

3 ____3 or more (2)   ____1 or 2 (1)   ____None

4 ____2 or more (2)   ____1 (1)   ____None

5 ____Over 10 (2)   ____Under 10

6 ____Over 1 hr (2)   ____Under 1 hr

7 ____2 or more (2)   ____Under 2

8 ____Over 1 hr daily (2)   ____Under 1 hr daily

9 ____Over 10 (2)   ____Under 10

10 ____Several times a week (2)   ____Rarely or never

11 ____Over 5 (2)   ____Under 5

12 ____Over 5 (2)   ____Under 5

13 ____Over 10 trips (2)   ____Under 10
A ____Over 3 trips (2)   ____Under 3

14 ____Much   ____Some (2)
A ____Always   ____Sometimes (1)   ____Never (2)

15 ____Very well (2)   ____Quite well (1)   ____Not well

16

A ____Gov't	____Media barons	
____Powerful interests		
____No one in particular (2)		
B ____Costly	____Cheap (2)	
C ____Often	Sometimes (1)	____Never (2)

Total: _____

Why is it important to be well-informed?

Information has *always* been important. Our cave-dwelling ancestors needed information about their environment to stay alive. Those who were not well-informed perished quickly.

Our world has grown more vast more complex more rapid more diffuse more discontinuous.

We need more and more information.

We need information to keep up with the rampage of change.

Information in more and more fields that impinge on our everyday lives.

Information about people across the planet whose lives increasingly interconnect with ours.

Information about older people among us who are living longer and longer and whose programmings and needs are often different from ours.

Information about younger people among us who are growing up in radically different worlds than we grew up in and whose wirings are different from ours.

Information about new complex machines that continually recontext all areas of our lives.

Information in an increasingly decentralized environment that demands everyone's input in new decision-making processes.

Information to protect ourselves from killer diseases that snuff out millions of lives every year. Information about diet and lifestyle—new medical technology—advances in genetics and life support systems—all of which can help extend our lives.

We also need information about information—its nature its power its uses and abuses.

Information is the lifeblood of our information age.

Who are the well-informed in today's world?

• *People with updated information*. In our age of rapid obsolescence information degrades quickly. In more and more fields textbooks remain valid no longer than a few months. There should be a recall of any diploma that is over ten years old. A Ph.D. or a master's degree earned twenty years ago simply means that you were trained for the world of twenty years ago. It does not attest to your competence in *today's* world. In our times the only valid diploma is update.

• *People with a multitrack information base*. In our world of convergent fields the specialist is at a disadvantage. The information rich is a specialist in many fields—a generalist. To be well-informed is to understand how information in any track fits into the total picture. For example to be an effective economist today you have to be updated on the regional economy—the global economy—world resources—new sources of energy—emerging technology—changing values—the dynamics of global telecommunication—global politics—the expanding Space environment—the biological revolution—the longevity revolution—etc.

• *People who receive their information from many sources*. Information that trickles down vertically from a fixed source or sources—such as a religious text or a specific political/national/ethnic/ideological source—has little value. Vertical information flow only reinforces existing biases. It is not open—interactive—evaluative. It lacks feedback and correctives. It disinforms.

To be information rich you have to tie in with the horizontal flow of information—information that flows from numerous disparate sources. Horizontal flow is open and self-refining.

- *People who process information intelligently.* To have an extensive information base does not automatically mean that one processes information well. "All facts and no bloody vision"—the late British parliamentarian Aneurin Bevan once said of a fellow party member. Processing information effectively (being well-informed) entails at least the following:
   —Jettisoning old information (prejudices—fixed ideas—emotionalism).
   —Learning from mistakes.
   —Distinguishing between information with short-range value and information with long-range impact.
   —Keeping the Big Picture in focus at all times. How does the new information fit into the total scheme of things (perspective).

Some people do all this automatically. They incorporate information intelligently. Others gobble up large quantities of information but do not ingest it well. Their information does not turn into knowledge. As a rule traditionalists—people who nurse the past—do not process information well. They use new information only to support hardened positions. In a rapidly changing world such people are poorly informed.

Why is it necessary to know English?

A command of "English" has become a prerequisite to being well-informed. I put the word English in quotes because I am not sure we should call it English any longer. In my book *Up-Wingers* (1972) I suggested we call English Unilang—universal language. English is now *the* global language and calling it Unilang may help defuse sensitivity to language dominance.

   —The fact is that English is now the official language in thirty-five countries.
   —It is used as a second language very nearly everywhere in the world. (It is taught at schools in the Soviet Union and China.)
   —It is spoken by around one billion people in the world—more than any other language. (Mandarin Chinese is second.)

—English itself is daily inundated with words from other languages—making it a truly global language.

—English is *the* language of global telecommunication—science—
technology—politics—trade. There is hardly a major development
or breakthrough in any field anywhere in the world that is not
instantly reported in English.

I find Italian—French—Portuguese—Russian more melodic and
pleasing to the ear than English. Italian in particular is the language of
paradise! But these are not global languages. Why then not adopt as
our common universal tongue the one that is already spoken by one out
of every five people on the planet?

A global language can help accelerate our evolution into a global
community—it can bring us together.

The fact is that if you only know Danish or Swahili or Urdu or
Vietnamese or any other *national* language—but do not know Unilang
well—you are in a communication brownout. You are not inflow.

Myths about the new information age.

Information flows in entirely new and unprecedented ways. We do not
yet fully understand the dynamics of this new information flow—how
it operates—how it recontexts—how it is altering the architecture of
our cultural and political and physical worlds. Some myths are carryovers from the oldworld of print. Here are some examples:

● *Myth #1: Information is controlled by special interests.*
Who controls information? No one. Some people may *briefly* control
some areas of communication. But no one and no organizations or
corporations or special interests or government can indefinitely control
any information.

The fear of ''controls'' is a legacy of the oldworld where in fact a
small number of people in each community or even nation did control
wealth and information and production.

But the new information—unlike the old—cannot be controlled—
monopolized or centralized.

People still *try* to control information. But information has grown too gigantic too multifaceted too rapid too personal too global too cumulative to be controlled for long. Information is everywhere.

Take the United States of America for example:

Half of the U.S. GNP is directly related to communication.

Half of the wages paid in the U.S. goes to people involved in the production—processing—distribution of information.

Nearly half of the jobs in this country are in "information occupations." (In the year 1900 only ten percent of all jobs were in this category.)

Some of the largest enterprises in America are information related: universities and schools—film industry—television—radio—telephone—computers—newspapers—magazines—book publishing—booksellers—libraries—data banks—advertising—etc.

The U.S.—the world's most powerful nation—lost the war in Vietnam chiefly because it lost the information war at home. (The tenacity of the Vietnamese obviously contributed to the American withdrawal.)

A recent American president was forced to resign from office for complicity in political tamperings. There is nothing new about this kind of chicanery. What is new is that in today's environment it is increasingly difficult to manipulate and squelch information—and get away with it.

In the 1970s and the 1980s the U.S. has had conservative administrations—yet during these years powerful movements spearheaded by women—students—consumers—environmentalists and others outside politics have brought about profound changes. Precisely because no one can control information.

World powers such as the USA and the Soviet Union are more powerful than ever—yet they continue to lose *relative* power and spheres of influence in the world. Precisely because they can no longer control information.

In technologically advanced societies a few people or corporations may still control a few radio and television stations—but they cannot control *all* radio and *all* television.

Can anyone or any corporation or administration or political group control the myriad sources of information: all films all television all radio all audio/visual cassettes and discs all direct satellite transmissions all computers all data bases all telephones all videoconferences all mail all books all magazines and telemagazines all advertising all desk-top printouts all newspapers all "foreign" films and press all tourists all "foreign" students and investors?

It is the *combination* of these and other information outlets that creates a powerful *information environment* that is increasingly difficult to control and manipulate.

The world is opening up—wider and wider. No one can close it down any longer. In one way or another the light is coming through.

- *Myth #2: It is costly to be information rich.*

In telespheral societies information is one of the cheapest and most abundant commodities.

While the price of industrial goods goes up—the price of information continues to go down.

Computations on a mainframe that cost a couple of dollars in the 1950s are now done for a fraction of a penny.

For a few pennies and a few minutes you can now use your computer from wherever you are to access information from thousands of free and commercial data bases in very nearly every field. In the industrial phase equivalent research takes a couple of *weeks* of library search.

For thirty cents you can buy a major global newspaper every day with updates of developments in many fields and major events all over the planet.

For around a hundred dollars you can buy a television set and for the next twenty years have a *front seat* at major global conferences—panel discussions—interviews with all kinds of people—festivals—exhibits. You can participate in seminars on world affairs—investments—health. You can watch close-ups of spacecraft liftoffs and landings—heart transplant and implant operations and other pioneering medical events. You can watch people milling around the Piazza San Marco in Venice or the marketplace in Ouagadougou. With the help of your TV set you can even lurk behind bushes and comfortably watch our primate ancestors and other animals going about their business in their natural habitats.

Soon a small inexpensive satellite dish will enable you to tune in TV channels in Rio de Janeiro and Marrakesh and Nairobi and Stockholm and Bucharest and Bombay and Bangkok and Sydney.

Today you can tune in these and other places around the planet with a push-button shortwave radio that costs no more than a couple of hundred dollars.

For a fraction of a dollar you can now call across the continental USA or Canada. If you don't talk long you can call across the planet for a couple of dollars.

In our times information degrades quickly. But the opportunities for quick continuous update are everywhere. It is easy and inexpensive to be information rich.

- *Myth #3: Watch out for information overload.*

There *is* no information overload. The human brain seems to have an infinite capacity to take in information. In fact the more information you take in the more you enlarge your brain's capacity to assimilate more information.

People who complain of information overload are in reality balking at the acceleration of *change*.

How Time Rich Are You?

1–How much time do you spend working?

    A–How many hours a day do you work?   ____7 & over   ____Under 6

    B–How many days a week?   ____5 & over   ____4 & under

    C–How many months a year?   ____Over 10   ____Under 10

2–Are you on a fixed work schedule or on flex time?   ____Fixed   ____Flex

3–Are you a workaholic? For example:

    A–How often do you go on working after your normal work hours?   ____Often   ____Sometimes   ____Never

    B–How often do you take work with you on vacation?   ____Often   ____Rarely

    C–Do you set the alarm to get up early on your days off?   ____Yes   ____No

    D–On free days do you cram the time with things to do?   ____Often   ____Sometimes

    E–Do you feel anxiety if you have a *totally free* unstructured day or week?   ____Yes   ____No

    F–Do you tend to overload—do many things at one time?   ____Often   ____Sometimes

    G–How often are you time pressured?   ____Often   ____Rarely

    H–How often are you close to burn-out?   ____Often   ____Rarely   ____Never

4–How leisurely is your life?

    A–How many leisure days do you have every week?   ____Over 3   ____1 or 2   ____None

    B–How often every year do you take off a *few days at a time* just to allow your system to idle?   ____Over 5 times   ____Under 5   ____Never

   C– Do you ever take off a year or two   ___Yes   ___No
         to coast and have fun: travel—
         play tennis—visit friends—etc.?

5– Do you think that life passes by very   ___Often   ___Sometimes
     quickly?   ___Never

Answer sheet: MONITOR 4

1

A	____7 & over	____Under 6 (2)
B	____5 & over	____4 & under (2)
C	____Over 10	____Under 10 (2)

2   ____Fixed   ____Flex (2)

3

A	____Often	____Sometimes (1)	____Never (2)
B	____Often	____Rarely (2)	
C	____Yes	____No (2)	
D	____Often	____Sometimes (2)	
E	____Yes	____No (2)	
F	____Often	____Sometimes (2)	
G	____Often	____Rarely (2)	
H	____Often	____Rarely (1)	____Never (2)

4 A	____Over 3 (2)	____1 or 2 (1)	____None
B	____Over 5 times (2)	____Under 5 (1)	____Never
C	____Yes (2)	____No	

5   ____Often   ____Sometimes (2)   ____Never (1)

Total: _____

Who are the time rich?

People who enjoy a nice *balance* in their use of time: fun time—free time—chore time—work time.

People who normally work fewer than five or six hours a day. Fewer than four days a week. Fewer than nine months a year.

People who do not take on many assignments or projects at one time.

People who are rarely—if ever—time-pressured. Rarely overcommitted or overextended.

People who do not work overtime and do not take work home.

People who can spend entire *free* days coasting—doing nothing that is generally considered "productive." For example: sleeping late—reading for pleasure—listening to music—watching television—making love—going for walks. Or just doing nothing.

People who take frequent vacations—just to have fun. Those who regularly drop out of the work track for a few days or a few weeks or a few months. Even for a year or two.

People who are on perpetual flex-time—seldom rushed.

People who pace their lives as though they were going to live for hundreds of years. (At such a leisurely pace they may very well end up living for hundreds of years.)

Why are workaholics ill-suited for the new environment?

● As a rule workaholics are one-dimensional. All they do is work. Such a work-intensive lifestyle—however gratifying to neurotic needs—is highly specialized and leaves large areas of intelligence and personality stunted. Workaholics are often boring because they run on a narrow track. All they know and all they talk about is their specific work. In our new environment which demands multifacetedness the workaholic is inefficient.

● Workaholics are rarely creative. They may be productive—but rarely creative. Leisure is indispensable to the flowering of creativity. (As I will explain later in this text creativity is a necessary asset in the postindustrial world.)

● In our age of rapid obsolescence continuous update is a precondition to growth. Workaholics never slow down long enough to update. Sooner or later this shows up in their work.

● Workaholics rarely live long. They are in hyperspeed and therefore burn out quickly—this at a time when people are living longer and longer.

When you overwork both the quality of your life and the quality of your work suffer.

"But I love my work. I don't even think of it as work."

I have a friend who is disdainful of the industrial age. He says he loves the telespheral world. He makes heavy use of automated office equipment and smart telecom systems—go-anywhere telephones—portable computers—videoconferences—etc.

There is a hitch. My friend is a workaholic. He works ten or eleven hours a day. Six or seven days a week. Even at social gatherings he talks about nothing but work.

"But I love my work—" he says. "I don't even think of it as work."

This is the workaholic's classical rationale. The fact is that if all you love is your work—if all you do is work—that makes for a one-dimensional life.

What is the benefit of deploying telespheral technology if your social values and work habits are still industrial age?

A work-intensive lifestyle is inherently outdated—no matter how updated the technology you use.

Workaholics are anachronisms in our times. They are carryovers from an earlier age when hard work was a prerequisite to survival and therefore considered a virtue.

Hard work is no longer necessary. We can produce more while working less and less.

In modern societies people who still work hard do so only because they do not manage their emotions and resources and time intelligently.

In our times of global surpluses and intelligent machines hard work is bad economics.

Compressed workweek—job sharing—flex time—temporary work —four-day workweek—these are all steps in the right direction.

We need to encourage people to work less and play more. Such a shift in emphasis will also help the "leisure industry" which not surprisingly is one of the explosive growth areas in the new economy.

The traditional yardsticks of success have been wealth—power— rank. The assumption has always been that the busier you are the more successful.

We need new yardsticks to measure success in the postindustrial world. Success in today's environment can be gauged by how much quality free time you have. The successful person today is one who has a balanced life of leisure/work/fun.

Does time really fly?

People who are always on the run never know where time goes.

The flow of time is in your hands. You can slow it down or speed it up.

People who live a well-paced leisurely life manage their own flow of time. They savor life.

To be rich in time is to be rich in the most precious resource in our universe.

How Fluid Are You?

	Strongly	Mildly	Hardly
1–Do you have a fixed or fluid identity? For example:			
A–Do you identify with your parents' ethnic origins?	—	—	—
B–Do you identify with your parents' nationality?	—	—	—
C–Do you identify with your parents' religion?	—	—	—

2–Should people hold on to their names even if they no longer identify with those names? ____Yes ____No

    A–Have you ever in your adult life formally changed your name or names (other than through marriage)? ____Yes ____No

3–How long have you lived your current lifestyle?

    A–For example: married—exclusive coupling—single—etc. ____Over 5 yrs ____Under 5

    B–Have you ever lived a fluid lifestyle: concurrent mix of single *and* couple *and* group living? ____Often ____Sometimes ____Never

    C–Do you consider a marriage or romance that lasts a few months or a couple of years a failure? ____Yes ____No

4–How many jobs have you held in the last ten years? ____More than 10 ____2 to 10

5–How long have you been in your current profession? ____Over 10 years ____Under 10

    A–How long in your previous profession? ____Over 10 years ____Under 10

6–How long have you been a member of your current political party?

    ____Over 10 yrs
    ____Under 10 yrs
    ____Independent

7–How many times have you changed residence (house—apartment—etc.) in the past ten years? (Include anything over a three-month stay.)

    ____Over 10 times
    ____3 to 10 times
    ____Under 3 times

8–How long have you lived in your present community (town—city—etc.)?

    ____Over 10 years
    ____Under 10 years

9–How many towns and/or cities have you lived in—over three months at a time?

    ____Over 10
    ____5–9   ____Under 4

10–How many countries have you lived in—over three months at a time?

    ____Over 10   ____5–9
    ____Under 4

11–How punctual are you?

    ____Very   ____Moderate
    ____Chronically tardy

12–Do you feel impelled to wake up at the same time—eat at the same time—sleep at the same time?

    ____Yes   ____No

13–How long do you hold on to grudges? For example:
    A–Do you forgive and forget and move on?

    ____Often   ____Sometimes
    ____Never

    B–Do you have long-standing prejudices toward specific groups: Blacks—Jews—Catholics—Arabs—or others?

    ____Yes   ____No

14–Do you think that the world is changing too fast?

    ____Too fast   ____Too slow
    ____About right

Answer sheet: MONITOR 5

	Strongly	Mildly	Hardly
1 A	——	——(1)	——(2)
B	——	——(1)	——(2)
C	——	——(1)	——(2)

2 ——Yes   ——No (2)
A ——Yes (2)   ——No

3 A ——Over 5 yrs   ——Under 5 (2)
B ——Often (2)   ——Sometimes (1)   ——Never
C ——Yes   ——No (2)

4 ——More than 10(1)   ——2 to 10 (2)   ——One

5 ——Over 10 years   ——Under 10 (2)
A ——Over 10 years   ——Under 10 (2)

6 ——Over 10 yrs   ——Under 10 yrs   ——Independent (2)

7 ——Over 10 times(1)   ——3 to 10 times (2)   ——Under 3 times

8 ——Over 10 years   ——Under 10 years (2)

9 ——Over 10 (2)   ——5–9(1)   ——Under 4

10 ——Over 10 (2)   ——5–9 (1)   ——Under 4

11 ——Very   ——Moderate (2)   ——Chronically tardy

12 ——Yes   ——No (2)

13 A ——Often (2)   ——Sometimes (1)   ——Never
B ——Yes   ——No (2)

14   ____Too fast   ____Too slow (2)   ____About right (1)

Total: _____

Who are the fluid in our times?

People who grow and move on—to new friendships new lifestyles new jobs new professions new communities new political philosophies new interests.

People who do not have fixed or static identities. In other words people who do not go through life perpetually defined by their origins—but who continually redefine themselves and are redefined in an increasingly discontinuous world.

People who change their names if they no longer identify with—or have outgrown—their given and inherited names.

People who flow in and out of different lifestyles or who enjoy a concurrent mix of lifestyles: single life *and* group living *and* coupling *and* networking.

People who are transglobal—who travel and live all over the planet and who are open enough to be reconditioned by new contacts.

People who are able to resolve conflicts quickly and move on. The extreme example of static personalities are those who marinate in grudges and enmities for years. Such people are stunted by their past and show little capacity for growth.

People who are energized by the acceleration of change in the world.

People who are well aware that there are no constant or eternal values and who therefore are free of dogmas.

What about commitment and loyalty?

Commitment and loyalty are undergoing profound transformations. At one time commitments and loyalties were passed on from one generation to the next. People *inherited* their commitments to tribe and clan—ancestral village or town—church—family profession—political affiliations.

Earlier in this century people began to outgrow *inherited* commitments. But they maintained lifelong commitments to a spouse—a profession—a community—a political movement—a nation.

In our fluid times commitments are loosening up even more. Commitments are increasingly concurrent and intermittent. In other words "fluid."

For example at one time people married in their teens and stayed together till they died of old age—at forty-five. As a rule a husband and a wife remained coupled—even if incompatible.

In today's hyperfluid environment people flow in and out of different or concurrent lifestyles. Intermittent coupling—quick linkup/linkouts—bicoastal rendezvous—singling—group living.

People seem to want choices and fulfillment.

A brief marriage or romance is no longer a failure. The failure lies in not understanding the changing rhythms of our new age.

The good news for people who like continuity in social ties is that friendships with ex-spouses and ex-lovers now go on forever.

(More on this theme in Monitor 15: Family.)

What about commitment to a profession?

At one time people embarked on a profession early in life and stayed with it till they retired or died. Changing jobs—much less professions—was considered irresponsible.

Today such continuity is not only difficult—it is not even desirable. The reasons are:

—A job or a profession that may have been stimulating to you at twenty-five may no longer be challenging at thirty-five—much less at forty-five.

—Because of rapid obsolescence your job may be phased out.

—For the same reason your entire profession may decompose.

—People are mobile as never before. You may want to shift orbits to another part of the country or planet and may not be able to find a job in your profession.

—People are living longer and longer. Can one remain stimulated in the same profession for fifty or sixty or seventy years?

To stay in any one job or profession too long—regardless of how well you do—often slows down growth. You may have a higher income and a more prestigious job but your potential for creativity may be reduced. And your organization will suffer from diminished circulation of fresh ideas.

Are all people who move around a lot fluid?

Not everyone who changes names—mates—lifestyles—professions—communities—ideologies is necessarily fluid.

Not everyone who travels around the planet is global. Not everyone who decouples frequently is liberated. Not everyone who changes jobs often is professionally fluid.

Not all change presumes growth.

Some people go through the mimings of change but change very little. Such changes may be escapist or cosmetic.

Changes reflect fluidity when there is a corresponding inner change and growth. Fluidity is growth.

The tightly wired.

"I have to wake up at seven every morning. I have to have lunch at twelve noon. I have to have dinner at seven P.M. I have to jog two miles every day. I have to arrive promptly at six for the cocktail party. I have to . . ."

People who live by perpetual deadlines often build up a lot of stress. We should expect such precision from our machines. We are not machines—not yet anyway.

I have rarely known rigidly structured people who enjoyed life. They are too busy mobilizing to meet their own inexorable deadlines.

I have rarely met a compulsively punctual person who was efficient.

People who are flex make more intelligent and fun use of time.

How High Tech Is Your Attention Span?

1–Do you stay at a job longer than five years?	____Yes	____No
2–Do you stay in your city or community for several weeks at a time without going away—or going crazy?	____Yes	____No
3–Do you write long letters—longer than one page?	____Often ____Sometimes ____Rarely	
4–Do you read books longer than 200 pages?	____Often ____Sometimes ____Rarely	
5–Do you read through long newspaper/magazine articles (over 2,000 words)?	____Often ____Sometimes ____Rarely	
6–Do you read documents—contracts —brochures—longer than three or four pages?	____Often ____Sometimes ____Rarely	
7–Can you sit through a play—any play?	____Yes	____No
8–Can you sit through a concert—at a concert hall?	____Yes	____No
9–Can you attend *every* session of a twelve- or fifteen-session seminar— on anything?	____Yes	____No
10–Do you balance your bank account every month?	____Yes	____No

11–Do you grow impatient when people talk in slow motion or go into unnecessary detail?

____Often   ____Sometimes
____Rarely

12–How often do you have telephone conversations that go on longer than twenty minutes?

____Often   ____Sometimes
____Rarely

13–Can you give the same presentation (lecture—speech—sales pitch—acting part) on more than five consecutive days?

____Yes   ____No

14–Can you enjoy the same cuisine (Italian—Chinese—Indian—etc.) more than twice in one week?

____Yes   ____No

15–How often do you play back your videotapes?

____Often   ____Sometimes
____Rarely

16–Do you see the same person (lover—friend—spouse) *every* evening for weeks at a time?

____Yes   ____No

Answer sheet: MONITOR 6

1 ____Yes   ____No (2)

2 ____Yes   ____No (2)

3 ____Often   ____Sometimes (1)   ____Rarely (2)

4 ____Often   ____Sometimes (1)   ____Rarely (2)

5 ____Often   ____Sometimes (2)   ____Rarely (1)

6 ____Often   ____Sometimes (2)   ____Rarely (1)

7 ____Yes   ____No (2)

8 ____Yes   ____No (2)

9 ____Yes   ____No (2)

10 ____Yes   ____No (2)

11 ____Often (1)   ____Sometimes (2)   ____Rarely

12 ____Often   ____Sometimes (2)   ____Rarely (1)

13 ____Yes   ____No (2)

14 ____Yes   ____No (2)

15 ____Often   ____Sometimes (2)   ____Rarely (1)

16 ____Yes   ____No (2)

Total: _____

Why is our attention span narrowing?

Our attention span is continually reset by a fast-response electronic environment.

In general our attention span corresponds to the pace with which we transmit information. The slower we exchange information the slower our attention span. The faster the exchange the more compressed our attention span.

We pick up the telephone and speedconnect across the country or planet. We turn on a switch and our computer terminal suddenly springs to life and begins to chatter away with other terminals all over the continent.

We activate our radio for instant news—instant interviews—instant updates—instant music—instant psychotherapy—instant medical diagnosis—instant sex advice.

Via remote control we produce a flush of quick fade-in/fade-out realities on our TV screens. We timeswitch and timefreeze and timescan. We flashback and flashforward.

Touch a button and switch years—decades—centuries. Switch from the 1980s to the 1830s to the 1460s to the 2030s. Just like that.

Touch a button and switch cities—countries—continents—planets. Switch from Boston 1996 to Beverly Hills 1936 to the South Seas 1870 to Vienna 1755 to Mars 2013. Just like that.

Touch a button and people-switch. Drop in on a global teleconference—eavesdrop on an intimate love affair—sit by safely and watch a realtime street demonstration across the planet.

You can even watch *several* events in different time zones *simultaneously*.

Soon even touch will be too slow. Just say the word and presto—switch contexts.

We tune in what we like—tune out what we do not like. Just like that.

We live in the age of instant access. Instant response. Instant tune-in/tune-out.

We receive and process and transmit information with a facility and rapidity unimaginable just a few decades ago.

Never have we juggled around time the way we do today.

This ability to shift contexts at will—to manipulate time—has profoundly compressed our attention span.

Specifically how has time compression resulted in attention compression?

We no longer sit down to write long letters. Why struggle with a long letter when you can pick up the telephone and interact? "Hi sweetheart—Here I am. Good to hear your voice. Are you free to-morrow night?"

Instant access. Instant response.

(Videophones and videocards will even supplant the postcard. Simply insert the videocard into your VCR and play it back live as often as you wish.)

We resist long books. By the time an idea or a story crystallizes in book form it has already played on television and radio and in magazines. Long books are hopelessly slow for our times. If an author cannot get it together in one or two hundred pages—forget it. The author is not addressing today's world.

More and more people refuse to sit still for three hours listening to a concert in a concert hall or listening to a long lecture. We are interactive generations conditioned by two-way feedback technology and brainstorming. We want to interact: talk back—sing along—jump up and down. One-way broadcast formats are increasingly out of sync.

People with high-tech attention spans have little patience for low-tech activities such as reading long documents or balancing monthly bank accounts.

More and more of us expect variety in *all* areas of our lives. Global TV introduces new people to us day and night. We have come to expect continuous sense-update. Seeing the same person or persons night after night overloads our circuitries.

A recent *New York Times* article titled " 'Lite' Decade: Less Has Become More" by William R. Greer alludes to this new fluidity.[1] "Sociologists say that 'lite' which started as a marketing term used to denote dietetic products, has become a metaphor for what Americans are seeking in disparate parts of their lives.

"In their relationships for example they have turned away from soul-searching and stress of emotional commitment . . . They seek light relationships.

"They can undergo psychoanalysis in one sitting because today's psychotherapy skips the formative years . . . Society wants current needs solved.

"That same lack of attachment is evident in the appliances people buy today . . . Appliances have become cheaper to replace than repair. They are light appliances—built to fall apart."

People also want "light literature, light shopping (by video), light politics, light responsibility . . . in the Light Decade, people not only want lite drinks and lite diet—they also want easy cures, easy jobs, easy riches. . . ."

Doesn't all this lightness and fastness lead to superficiality?

The yardsticks we use to judge quality come from slower times. People still tend to equate the detailed with the profound—the crisp and the light with the superficial.

We are impressed with bulk.

It ought to be axiomatic by now that a long intense marriage (particularly between two insecure people) is probably less profound than a light romance between two secure individuals.

A long book is not automatically more profound than a lean tract.

Television coverage is often dismissed as too rapid (instant think) and therefore shallow.

The problem is not that electronic media are too fast and therefore superficial. It is our thinking processes and communication protocols that are still slow.

A brief analogy may help illustrate this disparity. Agrarian (preindustrial) people as a rule take much longer to express themselves than a modern person. What may take an oldworld person twenty minutes to convey would take you no more than five minutes.

"May you never have a day such as I had last Tuesday—or was it last Wednesday—actually it was last Thursday—yes—last Thursday —the day we went to the marketplace. God protect you and your children—I was walking home with my son—not the one who works at the stables—but the one who worked for the chief—may God rest his soul—he was always good to all of us—we always remember him in our prayers. So I was walking home with my son—it was a little before sunset—or maybe . . ."

"Get to the fucking point!" you feel like shouting.

In the new electronic environment even print-oriented industrial-age people are slow. They exchange information at printpace.

Print uses more words and is slower than electronics. But it is not more profound. We are conditioned to think that it is.

People interviewed on television often express frustration at not having "enough time to explain." The problem is not with television. We have to learn to compress our thoughts more effectively. Electronic media such as TV and telephone demand a cohesion and organization of thoughts that print seldom does.

Electronic media are helping us rewire our way of communicating. They are helping us pare down and streamline. We are learning to say more in less time and with fewer words. We automatically edit out formalities and superfluities of slower times. We are more direct and cogent—often without our own awareness.

We are learning to shed verbal fat—not profundity.

Many years ago when interactive (talkback) radio and television came on line callers were embarrassingly clumsy. They hemmed and hawed and digressed before finally getting to the point. In time radio and TV helped listeners organize their thoughts and streamline their delivery. The result is that today's callers are far more succinct.

Speech compression—saying more with less—will continue to develop as electronics become more pervasive. Soon we will routinely dialogue with everyday machines. Later on we will converse with ultra-intelligent robots—androids—replicants. These new beings will not wait around. By the time you have finished saying "How do you do and how is your uncle?" they will have exchanged nine million bits of information.

By the year 2020 we will automatically say in a couple of minutes what now takes us fifteen minutes to convey. Our attention span will contract even more.

Doesn't such continued contraction of our attention span lead to a fast and tense world?

Fast yes—but not tense. The faster we exchange information the more quickly we attend to our needs and the more leisurely our lives.

As we grow more intelligent and our high-tech environment more smart our attention span will grow more efficient. We will have less and less patience for redundancies—superfluities—circumlocutions. We will exchange information more clearly and effectively. We will have bottom-line attention spans.

The faster our attention span the more leisurely our lives.

What Is Your Cultural Orientation?

	Often	Occasionally	Never
1–How often do you go to the opera?	——	——	——
2–How often to the theater?	——	——	——
3–How often to the ballet?	——	——	——
4–How often to art galleries?	——	——	——
5–How often to concert halls?	——	——	——
6–How often do you read "literature" (novels—poetry—etc.)?	——	——	——
7–How often do you go to the cinema?	——	——	——
A–How often to *new* cinema? (IMAX—180° films—Circle Vision)	——	——	——
8–How often do you watch television?	——	——	——
A–Do you watch large-screen TV?	——	——	——
B–Touch-and-enter interactive TV?	——	——	——
C–Videotapes via VCR?	——	——	——
D–Multiple-screen TV?	——	——	——
9–How often do you watch holographic or laser shows?	——	——	——

	Often	Occasionally	Never
10–How often do you watch space shows at observatories and planetariums?	___	___	___
11–How often do you attend videoart shows?	___	___	___
12–How often do you attend participatory music festivals?	___	___	___
A–How often participatory dance festivals?	___	___	___

Answer sheet: MONITOR 7

		Often	Occasionally	Never
1		____	____(2)	____(1)
2		____	____(2)	____(1)
3		____	____(2)	____(1)
4		____	____(2)	____(1)
5		____	____(2)	____(1)
6		____	____(2)	____(1)
7		____(2)	____(1)	____
	A	____(2)	____(1)	____
8		____(2)	____(1)	____
	A	____(2)	____(1)	____
	B	____(2)	____(1)	____
	C	____(2)	____(1)	____
	D	____(2)	____(1)	____
9		____(2)	____(1)	____
10		____(2)	____(1)	____
11		____(2)	____(1)	____
12		____(2)	____(1)	____
	A	____(2)	____(1)	____

Total: _____

What is old culture?

Old culture is old esthetics and old technology: opera—theater—ballet—literature—symphony hall concerts—paintings.

Old culture is rich with the cumulative output of recent centuries. Memorable sounds and dance movements and images and inspired writings are enshrined in this traditional culture.

These artistic and literary endeavors reflect the creative brilliance of countless artists and composers and choreographers and writers of recent centuries.

But this old culture has reached the end of the line. Its visions—values—rhythms—tools are largely outdated.

There is little innovation and originality in these old art forms.

This old culture is valuable because it tells us about our past and satisfies our nostalgia. People go to the opera the theater the ballet the art galleries—not because these cultural forms have something *new* to show us—but primarily because they playback the past. They evoke sounds and images and dance movements and stories of our childhood and worlds of our parents.

The old culture is a treasure house of memories.

Electronic culture.

A new electronic culture is coalescing from the new esthetics and values—the new technology—the new extraterrestrial environment.

The artists and scientists and visionaries of this emerging culture express new worlds through new tools: high-resolution giant screens—supercomputer imageries—synthesizers and sound mixers and lasers—zero-gravity simulations.

The sounds and images and dance movements they produce cannot be created through the old art mediums.

It is this new electronic culture that is attracting and galvanizing most of today's artistic innovation.

Once you have reveled in the larger-than-life sweep of IMAX and giant-screen cinema and touch-and-enter video—it is difficult to go back to the yestercentury confinements of opera and theater.

Once you have been swept away by the undreamed-of kaleidoscopic

imageries of videoart and videographics and special effects it is difficult
to find value in perpetuating still paintings.

Once you have been mesmerized watching people literally *dance in
the air* in zero gravity you can right away see how inherently clumsy
and labored *all* traditional and modern dances are.

Once you have dialogued with a supercomputer exchanging millions
of bits of information in seconds you will be appalled by the self-
indulgent sloppiness of a 500-page "literary" work.

Once you have awakened to the esthetics of a helicopter gyrating in
the air or a supersonic aircraft gliding across the sky or a spacecraft
storming the solar system it is perhaps easier to see that today's sculp-
tures are everywhere around us—out of the confinement of museums
and galleries.

Once you have listened to the limitless range of sounds and recom-
binations of sounds—worldly and cosmic—biologic and synthetic—
created with the help of computer seek-and-scan—synthesizers—light
induction—etc. it is easier then to realize how one-dimensional all
music—even great music—has been until now.

Once you have taken part in a global music festival—dancing and
singing with thousands of people—and tens of thousands of others on
giant-screen global TV hookups—it is difficult then to sit stiffly for
three hours dressed in tight formal attire in the hushed atmosphere of
a symphony hall for the very very serious business of listening to music.

The old culture was great in its time. But traditional culture does not
point the way to the future.

A new vigorous electronic culture is urgently crystallizing. It may
still at times be exploratory and undeveloped. But it signals magical
worlds ahead.

How Power Oriented Are You?

1–Do you believe in a god (an "almighty")?

____Yes   ____No

  A–Do you believe in messiahs and prophets with extraordinary powers?

____Yes   ____No

2–Are you drawn to the powerful or to the trappings of power? For example:

____Yes   ____No

  A–Do leaders have a certain mystique to you—regardless of their ideologies?

____Yes   ____No

  B–Do you like to be around people in authority: your boss— teachers—political leaders—etc.?

____Yes   ____No

  C–Do you tend to *automatically* support your leaders (corporate— religious—political)?

____Yes   ____No

3–Do you have heroes? (People you look up to or idolize.)

____Yes   ____No

4–How quick are you to advocate the use of force in dealing with intractable problems?

____Quick   ____Slow

5–Are you drawn to martial arts— boxing—hunting—bodybuilding?

____Yes   ____No

6–How often do you try to seek leadership positions in your organizations or groups?

____Often   ____Sometimes
          ____Never

7—Are you in a profession which inherently places you in a position of power over others?

    For example are you a teacher— psychotherapist—hypnotist— physician—politician—attorney —clergy—guru—counselor—police or military officer—etc.?
        ____Yes   ____No

8—How hierarchical are you? For example:

    A—Do you like clearly defined roles based on age or rank?   ____Yes   ____No

    B—Do you like to be addressed by your title and/or do you like to address others by their titles: "Doctor"—"Professor"— "Reverend" or "Father"— "Senator"—etc.?   ____Yes   ____No

9—Do you emphasize power and strength in everyday conversation: "the power of god"—"the most powerful nation on Earth"—"the need for strong leadership"—"he is a powerful person"?   ____Yes   ____No

Answer sheet: MONITOR 8

1   ____Yes   ____No (2)
  A ____Yes   ____No (2)

2   ____Yes   ____No (2)
  A ____Yes   ____No (2)
  B ____Yes   ____No (2)
  C ____Yes   ____No (2)

3   ____Yes   ____No (2)

4   ____Quick   ____Slow (2)

5   ____Yes   ____No (2)

6   ____Often   ____Sometimes (2)   ____Never (1)

7   ____Yes (1)   ____No (2)

8
  A ____Yes   ____No (2)
  B ____Yes   ____No (2)

9   ____Yes   ____No (2)

Total: _____

Who are the power oriented?

People who believe in gods and almighties and saviors.

People who struggle for control in social circles—organizations—church—government.

People who are drawn to professions that are normally power oriented: politics—business—medicine—psychotherapy—teaching—religion—etc.

People who are instinctively drawn to leaders and authority figures and the powerful. Often regardless of ideology.

People who emphasize the need for "strong leadership."

People who are quick to advocate the use of force in dealing with problems.

People who are attracted to firearms and to military parades and displays of military hardware.

People who are drawn to American football—boxing—martial arts—bodybuilding and other "sports" that emphasize strength and force.

People who have heroes and idols.

People who rationalize wrongdoings of a leader by ascribing blame to those around him or her.

People who like hierarchy: titles—ranks—pecking orders.

People who are in awe of those in authority or in the limelight: politicians—physicians—gurus—athletic champions—celebrities.

People who frequently talk about "power" and "might" and "strength."

Where does power fixation come from?

The attraction to power is universal. Probably everyone has some vestigial awe of and attraction to power.

Is this veneration of power (authority—leadership—strength) an outgrowth of our childhood dependence on the power of our all-protective parents? If this is the case then it is easy to see why the powerful (gods and leaders and others) are comforting to so many adults. Power is unconsciously identified with survival. Power means protection.

The pathological veneration of power may have been reinforced early in our evolution by the survival-need for dominant pack leaders (such as among primates) and still later absolute tribal leaders. In the primitive setting autocratic leadership with its centralization of authority may have been the most expedient way to cope with threats of a hostile environment.

Much of the present glorification of leaders and "hail to the chief" in *all* societies may be a direct throwback to our earliest tribal days.

Are we moving toward more or less concentration of power?

The trend in the world is away from power. We are steadily moving toward the decentralization of power—at all levels of all societies. This process is obviously more evident in postindustrial societies.

In the United States and Canada for example the following deviations from centralization of authority are evident:

—Entire generations are growing up in reciprocal home environments with little of the authoritarian parenting of the oldworld. These generations are growing up less in awe of authority than any previous generations—less inclined to hero worship—less power-oriented—less and less obsessed with leading or needing to be led. This trend is already evident in youngsters' confident interactions with parents—teachers—other authority figures.

These consensus generations cannot later be conditioned to fear authority. To them power will never have a mystique.

—Information has been one of the tools that has helped the powerful to monopolize power. The more centralized the sources of information the more powerful the centers of authority (family—church—government—etc.). Thanks to the proliferation of modern communication technology information now flows in new ways. In telespheral societies in particular nearly everyone has access to information. You don't have to go to the teacher for information or to the clergy or the employer or the scientist or the government leaders. Simply activate one of the many print or electronic outlets around you and the information will pour out—as though out of a Niagara.

People have not yet learned to access this new abundance. But it is just a matter of time.

For example computers now enable individual workers to obtain instant updates on all areas of production and assist them in decision making. Information that at one time was available only to managers is now available to everyone. The new technology opens the way for self-management reducing the need for hierarchy.

Because of this confluence of psychological and informational factors (as well as the spread of affluence) people are less and less submissive to and dependent on authority. There are still flagrant imbalances in power everywhere. But the trend is toward reciprocity.

Isn't the central government growing bigger and more powerful particularly in modern technological societies such as the U.S.?

As information decentralizes the relative power of governments decline. As communication grows more powerful people grow more powerful —governments lose power.

In a communication-intensive environment government leaders are more exposed to public scrutiny and censure than ever. More vulnerable to public pressure.

This is particularly evident in telespheral societies such as the United States where the government increasingly reacts to pressures for change that build up outside the political arena.

Since the early 1960s the most profound transformations in the United States have been spearheaded and sustained by people *outside* government. For example the civil rights movement—the women's movement—the sexual liberation—the consumer crusade—the biological revolution—the environmental movement—the leisure ethic—the workers' participation movement—the peace movement.

These and other movements have generated vast social—economic —political changes.

No less noteworthy is the fact that these upheavals unfolded during successive conservative administrations of the 1970s and the 1980s that were largely opposed to these movements.

The point here is that government no longer always sets the pace and is less and less effective in stopping or slowing down the massive recontextings going on everywhere.

Those who still look to government as the principal driving force for progress do not understand the new realities of postindustrial society.

There have been no "strong leaders" in the United States (and West European countries) in recent decades mainly because the decentralized environment is not hospitable to "strong leaderships."

The U.S. presidency may be more visible than ever and there may be more pomp and pageantry surrounding it. But this must not be confused with power.

The American presidency is slowly evolving into a ceremonial position—like the monarchies in West European countries. By the second or third decade of the new century presidential elections in the U.S. will probably have about as much significance as today's Academy Awards. Thanks to national television presidential elections will probably grow more glitzy—but they will have less and less substance.

In fact national elections in the U.S. and other technologically advanced nations are already less and less reflective of the ideological mood of the country.

The long-range direction is toward electronic democracy: public opinion polls—referendums—"direct legislation" via ballots and propositions. In other words voting on issues—not for individuals. (For more on this please see Monitor 20: Ideology. Also my book: *Telespheres*.)

Who then are the most "powerful" people in a country such as the U.S.?

This is increasingly an anachronistic question.

The powerful are no longer only those in traditional positions of power: government leaders—corporate heads—press lords—media executives. The powerful are also the millions of people whose daily cross-fertilization helps create new *information environments* that make it possible to bring about change.

In a sense then everyone in a postindustrial society is powerful.

The major catalyst is telecommunication—which is in everybody's hands. Everyone is pushing buttons.

What about titles and rank and other trappings of hierarchy?

"Titles flatter the mediocre and embarrass the really gifted"—wrote George Bernard Shaw.

The new technology is playing havoc with hierarchy. Neither the mediocre nor the really gifted need to be embarrassed.

How Competitive Are You?

	Often	Sometimes
1–Do you speak in competitive terms? For example:		
A–"He is the most brilliant man here." "This is the best country in the world."	____	____
B–Do you use such terms as "She is a winner." "He is a loser"?	____	____
C–Do you emphasize awards: "He is a Nobel Prize winner." "She is a two-time Pulitzer Prize winner"?	____	____
D–Do you tend to grade: "This concert was a six." "She is a nine"?	____	____

2–Is it important to you to "win" discussions?	____Yes	____No
A–Is it important to you to prove that you are right?	____Yes	____No

3–How rivalrous are you with your siblings (brothers and sisters)? Your parents? Offspring? Friends? Colleagues?	____Very	____Mildly

4–Do you emphasize grades in your studies?	____Yes	____No
A–Do you push (your) children to aim for high grades?	____Yes	____No

5–Do you like to *compete* in games and sports?	____Yes	____No
A–Do you keep score?	____Yes	____No
B–Do you play to win or to have fun?	____Win ____Fun	____Both

6–Do you enjoy watching competitive sports?
____Yes   ____No

A–Does it matter to you who wins?
____Yes   ____No

7–Do you compete in or enjoy watching such events as Academy Awards—Emmy Awards—beauty contests—TV talent contests—music competitions—etc.?
____Yes   ____No

8–Are you overjoyed when someone close to you wins a competitive event?
____Yes   ____No

9–Do you feel sad for *anyone* who loses a competitive event (other than friend or home team)?
____Yes   ____No

10–How important is it to you to be "No. 1" in your field?
____Important
____Not important

A–Do you admire people or groups that strive to be No. 1?
____Yes   ____No

B–Does it matter to you whether or not your country is No. 1 in any area?
____Yes   ____No

11–Is competition a good thing—a stimulus to growth?
____Yes   ____No

Answer sheet: MONITOR 9

		Often	Sometimes	
1	**A**	____	____ (2)	
	B	____	____ (2)	
	C	____	____ (2)	
	D	____	____ (2)	
2		____Yes	____No (2)	
	A	____Yes	____No (2)	
3		____Very	____Mildly (2)	
4		____Yes	____No (2)	
	A	____Yes	____No (2)	
5		____Yes	____No (2)	
	A	____Yes	____No (2)	
	B	____Win	____Fun (2)	____Both
6		____Yes	____No (2)	
	A	____Yes	____No (2)	
7		____Yes	____No (2)	
8		____Yes	____No (2)	
9		____Yes (2)	____No	
10		____Important	____Not important (2)	
	A	____Yes	____No (2)	
	B	____Yes	____No (2)	
11		____Yes	____No (2)	

Total: _____

Is competition a spur to human progress?

There is an old myth that competition helps us move forward. The fact is that we have advanced to this stage not because we have had to compete—but mainly because we have had to cooperate.

We compete because we are too dumb to know any better.

Unable to outgrow competitiveness we have—in desperation—glorified and institutionalized it. We have made a virtue out of a crude wasteful behavior that goes back to our earliest primate origins.

Today more than ever competition is divisive and inefficient. In the age of nuclear overkill competition can be downright suicidal.

How and why is competition antifuture?

—Competition fosters an adversarial atmosphere that often leads to stress and a host of diseases—including fatal heart attacks.

In their pioneering book *Type A Behavior and Your Heart* Dr. Meyer Friedman and Dr. Ray M. Rosenman[1]—two cardiologists—note that ninety-eight percent of heart attack victims score high on the "Type A" rating scale. Type A behavior is described as competitive—driven—aggressive—achievement-oriented. Some typical Type A characteristics:

- Scheduling more and more activities into less and less time.
- Becoming unduly irritated when driving behind a car you think is moving too slowly.
- Making a fetish of always being on time.
- Having difficulty sitting and doing nothing.
- Playing nearly every game to win—even when playing with children.

The cardiologists point out that much of the socialization in America fosters Type A patterns—for example the belief that you have to be No. 1.

It is not difficult to see how antisurvival competition is. What is the good of beating out others—being a winner—if the result is that you are driven to alcoholism or drugs—ulcers—back problems—or dropping dead of a heart attack at the age of forty-two?

—Highly competitive individuals are so mobilized to beat out rivals that they hardly have time to broaden their interests and skills. In a world of interdependent disciplines this overspecialization soon affects the quality of their performances.

Common examples are highly driven musicians—actors—dancers—athletes—business people—attorneys. They are all so obsessed with winning that they block out everything else. The result is the one-dimensional person with whole areas of personality and intellect conspicuously undeveloped.

Spend an afternoon with a high-powered attorney or corporate executive or physician who makes say two hundred thousand dollars a year. You will be dazzled with this person's specialized competence. But shift to any other field and you will be dumbfounded by this person's barrenness.

A classical example is the tennis player John McEnroe. Here is a person so obsessed with winning that he is often driven to pathetic tantrums and abuse during matches.

How valuable is competition when it stunts our emotional and intellectual growth? What price winning?

—Highly competitive people rarely even enjoy what they do. For example youngsters who are pushed to excel in music often end up hating music. Students pressured to get good grades at school may never develop the joy of learning.

"How are your youngsters doing at school?"

"My son is straight A's. My daughter had three A's and two B's."

Why tell me their grades? I just wanted to know if they are *enjoying* their education and what they are learning.

"How was your tennis today?"

"Terrible. I lost two out of three sets."

Damn it. Did I ask you for the score? Did I ask you whether you won or lost? I just wanted to know if you *enjoyed* the tennis or had a good workout.

We have forged fiercely competitive environments that foster counterproductive motivations. Not the joy of playing or learning or growing or creating. But the drive to beat out others.

When people succumb to the pressures of competition and cheat to win or throw tantrums or get drunk we ostracize them.

—Competition is particularly inefficient because it leads to duplication. Scores of research centers compete fiercely to develop a cure for a disease. Often they all go through the same expensive time-consuming research. How much more quickly cures would be found if they all collaborated.

Such wasteful duplication exists within and among organizations—corporations—government agencies—nations.

In politics several candidates with indistinguishably similar ideologies will compete for a specific office. If these people were genuinely interested in promoting their agenda—rather than themselves—they would designate one candidate to represent their ideology and the others would lend support.

It is chiefly because we compete and do not collaborate enough that many age-old problems are still with us—for example undernourishment and poverty. If we competed less and collaborated more we could insure abundance for all—we could all enjoy more leisure—we could more rapidly find ways to extend the human life span. When we say that "politics" stand in the way what we often mean is that competitiveness stands in the way.

Far from stimulating progress competition actually slows it down.

Doesn't competition encourage the "best" in society to surface and in so doing promote general welfare?

This is a fallacy. What is generally considered the "best" or "number one" is often the mediocre. What has the greatest appeal to the greatest number of people is rarely "the best" that a society produces.

In creating a competitive environment we allow the people and the products with the greatest mass appeal to rise to the top. We mistake popularity for quality. We set up false standards that undervalue those qualities (such as creativity and originality) that most stimulate progress.

It is often the mediocre student who gets straight A's. The truly gifted creative student is usually bored with school and rarely gets good grades.

It is often the mediocre bureaucrat who rises to the top. People who are imaginative and have original ideas rarely become corporate heads.

It is often the mediocre film that wins the Academy Award. Often the mediocre TV program that wins Emmys. Films and TV programs that break new ground often cannot find distributors and rarely win recognition.

It is often the mediocre book that wins awards and lands on best-seller lists. Seminal or avant-garde books often cannot find publishers and if published rarely gain recognition right away.

In the field of futurism (long-range planning) the few books that land on best-seller lists are not—as one would expect—books that have anything new to present. Rather they are books that skillfully package ideas that have been around a dozen years or more.

It is often the mediocre who become presidents and prime ministers and cabinet members and senators and governors and mayors and judges. People with high intelligence and high ideals do not as a rule subject themselves to the crass machinations inherent in running for political office.

Take the United States for example: can you think of more than two or three U.S. presidents during the entire twentieth century who had above average intelligence?

Turn off the blinding spotlights and what you will find are some ordinary individuals. Driven and ambitious—but ordinary.

When people here say that in America any youngster can grow up to become president what they are really saying is that in America anyone can rise to—mediocrity.

I have no quarrel with mediocrity. Mediocrity is part of the process. The mediocre help implement advances brought on by progressive forces.

My quarrel is with the myth that competition stimulates progress. Competition promotes mediocrity.

The driving forces of human progress are creativity—originality—imagination—inventiveness. These are not attributes that usually win popularity contests or are touted as the "best."

If we do not have competition how can we ever know who is best—really best?

Why do we ever need to know who is best in anything?

Why do we ever need to know who is the most beautiful—the most intelligent—the most successful—the most talented?

Why do we ever need to know who is the brightest—the fastest—the strongest—the sexiest— the richest?

Why do we ever need to know what the best film is or the best TV show or the best book or the best music or the best restaurant or the best country?

Why do we constantly pit people against one another?

Why do we have to have winners and losers?

For every winner we create scores of losers. For no reason at all.

This relentlessly competitive environment serves no useful purpose. Above all it proves nothing.

The fact is that there is no such thing as the "best." There is no such thing as the most attractive—the most intelligent—the most talented.

There is no such thing as the best performer. No best director. No best writer. No best architect. No best physicist. No best pianist or violinist.

There is no best anything.

Most human activities cannot be quantified for accurate comparisons.

Then too this obsession with ratings trivializes everything. We trivialize learning—trivialize intelligence—trivialize creativity—trivialize science and art and business and politics and sports. We trivialize human relations.

The annual Academy Awards presentations highlighted with much fanfare on global television are an example of the trivialization of creativity and entertainment.

Hundreds of actors—directors—producers—others involved in the making of films attend these ceremonies in formal clothes. (Perhaps the no-nonsense attire is intended to lend some sophistication to this basically aggressive vulgar affair.) Awards for the "best" this and the "best" that are bestowed and ravenously accepted with pathetic melodrama.

This offensive annual display unleashed on the world trivializes the lovely magical world of cinema.

Why reduce everything to competition? Why childrenize and manipulate people by bestowing and denying rewards?

One day in the coming decades—as we evolve into more intelligent people—we will look back with embarrassment at such imbecile affairs as the Academy Awards—the Emmy Awards—the Nobel Prize Awards—the Olympic Games—the Miss Universe Contest . . .

Praise and reinforcement are certainly necessary. But why at the expense of others?

It is one thing to say "You are an admirable scientist" (or artist or whatever). It is quite another thing to proclaim to the world that "You are the *best.*"

Decades ago psychologists made us aware of the injuriousness of pitting siblings against one another. Enlightened parents stopped the age-old habit of manipulating their children by comparing them with one another: "Your sister is prettier than you. Your brother is much smarter than you will ever be. . . ."

If it is obvious to us now that such manipulative parenting undermines the self-confidence of children and engenders lifelong aggressiveness and bitterness why do we persist in perpetuating such competitiveness in other areas of our lives?

Some people in California have created noncompetitive games and sports. The object of these activities is to help people collaborate— rather than compete—to keep a game going. We have introduced such no-lose games to our Futurist picnics in Los Angeles. They have been fun and stimulating.

We all need to incorporate this collaborative spirit in all areas of our activities.

Isn't the whole world competitive? Why single out Americans?

It is said that New Yorkers were very disappointed recently when they learned that their city is the *second* dirtiest in the world. They always like to be No. 1.

Americans certainly did not *invent* competition. People the world over have been competitive since the days we swung from trees. For example the Soviet Union which attempts to deemphasize competition in many phases of its socialized economy is nevertheless a highly competitive society. Contests pervade all areas of Soviet life: piano competitions—ballet competitions—literary contests—chess contests. Soviet and other East European athletes are encouraged—and heavily subsidized—to train for Olympic and other international competitions. How ironic that socialist societies that strive to protect their people from survival-of-the-fittest economics nevertheless hound them to beat out others in endless competitions.

Americans on the other hand have popularized competition by packaging all kinds of activities into money-making competitive enterprises: beauty pageants—talent contests—quiz programs—televised award presentations—even fiercely fought lucrative political campaigns that drag on for a year or two.

Impressionable people around the planet have imported these glamorized competitive packages—raising the stress level in their societies.

America has been a creative—innovative—progressive society not because of its capitalist glorification of competition—but mainly because of the cross-fertilization and collaboration of millions of people of diverse cultures.

MONITOR 10
How Affluent Are You?

1–Are you wealthy? (in the U.S. households earning more than $200,000 per year)

____Yes ____No

2–Are you affluent? (more than $50,000 per year)

____Yes ____No

3–Are you part of the "working majority"—not well-off but modestly comfortable? (more than $25,000 a year for single person—more than $35,000 for family of four)

____Yes ____No

4–Are you poor? (less than $6,000 per year for single person—less than $11,000 a year for family of four)

____Yes ____No

5–Are you part of a family or network of friends that shares resources enabling you to upgrade your life?

____Yes ____No

6–Can one *live* a modern life—high values and high-tech—on low income?

____Yes ____No

7–Do you have resistances to affluence? For example:

A–Do you feel that you deserve to struggle and be poor?

____Yes ____No

B–Do you think there is too great an emphasis on material possessions?

____Yes ____No

C–Do you feel guilty about your affluence?

____Often ____Sometimes ____Never

8–Are you a liberated rich? For example:

A–Do you have much leisure time: work *less* than six hours a day—four days a week—eight or nine months a year? ____Yes ____No

B–Do you have runaway retreats? ____Yes ____No

C–Do you sometimes use a helicopter to commute? ____Yes ____No

D–Is your work creative or challenging? ____Yes ____No

E–Are your home and work environments high-tech? ____Yes ____No

F–Do you often travel for pleasure? ____Yes ____No

G–Is there much gaiety in your life? ____Yes ____No

H–Do you generously share your affluence? (gifts—treats—conviviality—donations—contributions—support for your ideals) ____Yes ____No

Answer sheet: MONITOR 10

1   ____Yes (2) ____No

2   ____Yes (2) ____No

3   ____Yes (1) ____No

4   ____Yes   ____No

5   ____Yes (2) ____No

6   ____Yes   ____No (2)

7   **A**   ____Yes   ____No (2)
     B   ____Yes   ____No (2)
     C   ____Often   ____Sometimes (2)   ____Never (1)

8   **A**   ____Yes (2) ____No
     B   ____Yes (2) ____No
     C   ____Yes (2) ____No
     D   ____Yes (2) ____No
     E   ____Yes (2) ____No
     F   ____Yes (2) ____No
     G   ____Yes (2) ____No
     H   ____Yes (2) ____No

Total: _____

Who are the liberated rich?

People who can afford to have high values and high-tech.
  People who rarely have to compete for anything.
  People who seldom rush—who are perpetually flex.
  People who rarely experience stress.
  People who only do work they love—at their own pace—in their own way—with compatible collaborators.
  People who live close to their ideals.
  People who have the resources and the time to give generously to the world.
  People who are always teleconnected via onbody telecom.
  People who helicopter on short treks—supersonic on long hauls.
  People who have many attractive liftoff/landing pads: apartments in the city—houses in the country—hotels—resorts—Club Meds—cruises.
  People who translive in a global environment: global network of friends and associates—global teleconferencing—global travel—global overview—global loyalties.
  People who can on short notice rendezvous with friends or lovers— anywhere on the planet. "How about dinner in Saint Tropez tonight?"
  People with a psychology of abundance. People who are well aware of the abundance in the universe and who live a life of abundance: abundant time—abundant resources—abundant growth—abundant creativity—abundant generosity—abundant fun.
  Today's liberated rich are forerunners of twenty-first-century people.

Who are the slow-growth poor?

The wealthy who live modestly and share nothing. They might as well be poor. Theirs is a stagnant wealth. Wealth without joy. Wealth without growth.
  People who think poor. Those who always talk about scarcity and limits to growth and deficits and overruns and sacrifices.
  The chronically poor in affluent societies. People with obvious talents who remain poor because of guilt about affluence—deflated self-image—self-denial—pathological dependency on others—unwillingness to give—or just unintelligent management of personal life.

Can one have high values and high-tech on low income?
In other words can one be poor and enjoy a progressive life?

You cannot live a modern life on a premodern income.

You cannot be poor and live a progressive life.

If you are chronically poor you will inevitably remain trapped in yesterday values and lifestyles. You will not be able to create an environment that will allow you to be noncompeting—generous—leisurely—fluid—mobile—global—diversified—fulfilled.

If you are chronically poor you are probably also time poor. You are black-holed in a struggle for survival and can hardly be creative and innovative.

If you are chronically poor you inevitably deploy yesterday technology. A low-tech environment invariably means drudgery—monotony—hard-work—waste—sacrifice.

Poverty slows down growth: psychological—social—intellectual—economic—political. Poverty is regressive.

Affluence is progressive.

How can I live a modern life if I do not have independent resources and am unwilling to work hard and compete to make money?

Traditionally when people have needed financial assistance for college or a new car or a better house—they have gone to the family.

If family is not a viable support for you there is an alternative—a Network of Friends. If you do not have the money or the income to upgrade your life create a Network of Shared Affluence.

For example if you cannot afford an attractive place of your own pool resources with two or three or more people and rent or buy an attractive apartment or house. This is called Shared Housing and more and more people of all ages are doing it.

If you need to drop out of work for a while but cannot afford to do so improvise arrangements with two or more friends. Take turns supporting one another while each takes time off to coast or travel or study or recharge batteries. (Two-income homes are doing this—why not a four-income network?)

If you have a good income but still cannot afford your own helicopter—share one. More and more people are doing this.

If you cannot afford your own runaway house in the country combine resources with others and rent such a place. Tens of thousands of people are already doing this in Hawaii and California and the Hamptons (on Long Island/New York) and in the Caribbean and on the French Riviera.

Sharing and networking and bartering are the waves of the future.

Create Networks of Shared Affluence.

Why is affluence the way of the future?

"Let me first remind you of the obvious"—wrote John M. Keynes the English economist during the depth of the Great Depression. "The large mass of population in the world is living much better than ever."

The farther back we go in history the poorer we *all* were. The more we advance into the future the more affluent more and more of us grow.

By the standards of 1850 very nearly everyone in a postindustrial society today is affluent. By the standards of 2050 everyone today is poor—even the wealthy.

Everywhere in the world people are better off today than ever. This is clearly reflected in hard statistics:

Lowest infant mortality in history.

Lowest adult mortality everywhere in the world.

Highest life expectancy everywhere.

Greatest surplus of food in the world.

Slowest rate of population growth in decades.

More telecommunication hardware—even in poor countries.

More people traveling voluntarily around the planet (1.3 billion annually).

If at times it appears that some less developed areas are sliding or standing still—it is because we regard those areas from the vantage point of late twentieth century. Even the poorest countries are making headway. If you have any doubts contact an information outlet—for example the United Nations library—and obtain playbacks of where these societies were thirty or forty years ago.

Still there is much poverty in our world. Even one single under-nourished person anywhere is one too many.

Anyone who knows the compositions of our continents and oceans and the solar system and the galaxies knows full well that we live in a universe of limitless abundance.

There is still poverty in the world not because of scarce resources—but because we haven't yet developed the psychology and the economics to tap the cornucopia around us.

It is like living on a huge estate overflowing with provisions and riches—yet fighting over the limited provisions in one tiny storeroom.

How ridiculous to fester in poverty and recessions and inflations amid all this glut of resources.

There is no scarcity. Only a psychology of scarcity. Only an infra-structure of scarcity.

But we are steadily breaking out of these anachronistic loops.

We are moving toward more and more abundance. My projection (first made in the 1960s) is that by around the third decade of the new century all *real* poverty will have phased out. All humanity—wherever we are—will enjoy abundance.

How will this come about?

Limitless cheap energy: solar—fusion—hydrogen fuel—etc.

Limitless raw materials: from the oceans—earth's interiors—moons—planets—asteroids.

Limitless time: indefinite life spans.

Limitless space: solar system and beyond.

Limitless vision: postscarcity and postpuritan *psychology* of abun-dance.

We have enough resources to insure abundance for every one of us for millions and billions of years. Abundance for as long as there is a universe.

How Ritualistic Are You?

1–Do you observe birthdays? (your own and/or others) ____Yes   ____No

2–Do you enjoy attending wedding ceremonies? ____Yes   ____No
  A–Engagements? Showers? ____Yes   ____No

3–Do you observe anniversaries? (your own and/or others) ____Yes   ____No

4–Do you observe mourning rituals when someone close to you dies? (religious services—staying at home—wakes —graveside visits—wearing black) ____Yes   ____No

5–Do you observe Mother's Day and Father's Day? ____Yes   ____No

6–Do you observe national holidays? For example:
  A–Do you watch or participate in parades—street festivities—fireworks? ____Yes   ____No
  B–Do you display the flag? ____Yes   ____No

7–Do you observe religious holidays? For example:
  A–Christmas tree? Christmas cards? Gift exchanges? ____Yes   ____No
  B–New Year's Eve celebration? ____Yes   ____No
  C–Turkey dinner on Thanksgiving? ____Yes   ____No
  D–Do you go to a place of worship (church—temple—mosque—etc.) on major religious holidays? ____Yes   ____No

8–Do you observe religious and/or social initiation events?

    A–Communion? Christening? Bar mitzvah?   ___Yes   ___No

    B–Debutante's ball? Coming-out party?   ___Yes   ___No

Answer sheet: MONITOR 11

1 ____Yes   ____No (2)

2 ____Yes   ____No (2)
 A ____Yes   ____No (2)

3 ____Yes   ____No (2)

4 ____Yes   ____No (2)

5 ____Yes   ____No (2)

6 A ____Yes   ____No (2)
 B ____Yes   ____No (2)

7 A ____Yes   ____No (2)
 B ____Yes   ____No (2)
 C ____Yes   ____No (2)
 D ____Yes   ____No (2)

8 A ____Yes   ____No (2)
 B ____Yes   ____No (2)

Total: _____

Why rituals?

You can tell a lot about a culture by what it celebrates. Cultures that are past-oriented have numerous rituals and ceremonies marking past events: births and deaths and martyrdoms of prophets and saints as well as observances of regional and national historic events.

The oldworld was awash in rituals. Religious and tribal and national ceremonies helped formalize and structure life. They also helped lend color to otherwise drab and uneventful existences.

Life in preagrarian and agrarian times was a relentless struggle for survival. People toiled hard—six or seven days a week—year after year. Holidays were therefore welcome respites. People wore their "Sunday suits" and went out to celebrate or attend ceremonies at places of worship.

As we grow more fluid our need for rituals diminishes. Birthdays and anniversaries—national and religious holidays lose their appeal. People are less impelled to repeat obligatory formulas year after year —Merry Christmas. Happy New Year. Happy birthday. Happy . . .

Modern people's celebrations are increasingly based on voluntarism and spontaneity rather than automatic adherence to repetitive abstractions. They may for example celebrate the completion of a project— the start of a new endeavor—the joys of an ongoing romance or friendship—a new partnership—a new home.

To most modern people very nearly every day is a delight. They are out in the evenings having fun: parties—movies—shows—discotheques—restaurants—rendezvous with friends and lovers. Weekends are often spent away—on trips or at runaway country houses.

We take all this for granted and forget that by standards of traditional societies we are astonishingly hedonistic.

In our postpuritan times there is nothing special about Christmas or New Year's or other traditional holidays. Every day is special.

Birthdays.
Birthdays are narcissisms left over from our childhoods. Future-oriented people are born and reborn every day. Every day is a liftoff. Every day a new beginning.

Wedding ceremonies.

These are rituals that allow two people to announce to the world that they now "belong" to each other. Weddings would be more honest if the bride and bridegroom peed on each other to establish their territory. "Keep out everybody—this is now my property."

Mother's Day and Father's Day.

For people who are usually mean to or dismissive of their parents— such observances allow them the opportunity to be nice for at least one day. They can then revert to their habitual patterns the rest of the year.

Imagine how many more businesses would prosper if we also had Daughter's Day and Son's Day and Brother's Day and Sister's Day and Aunt's Day and Pet's Day. . . .

Anniversaries.

I was invited to an anniversary party not long ago. Everyone went around saying how wonderful it was that the guests of honor had been married to each other for fifty years. Fifty years.

"My wife and I have been married for fifty years," the husband said proudly in his speech. "We have never been apart. We are very proud of what we have accomplished."

Everybody gave them a standing ovation.

The thought flashed on my screen: This is probably the last generation to celebrate a fiftieth wedding anniversary. In the coming years living with the same person—day in day out—for fifty years will seem as odd as living in the same house for fifty years or staying at the same job for fifty years.

Religious holidays.

In the cities of North America and Europe around Christmas and other major holidays tens of thousands of singles suffer from "holiday depression." These people have no families to spend certain holidays with.

Their mistake is that they try desperately to fit yesterday's traditions into today's realities. One of these days they will have a consciousness shift. The realization will at last register that they are no longer little children in 1948 or 1955 or 1969—that they have outgrown family and religion and do not need to celebrate holidays. All they have to do is go out and do what they do so well with their friends all year long— have fun.

National holidays.

National holidays are vulgar affairs that celebrate an anachronism—the nation.

Every country still goes through the same self-congratulatory ritual on these holidays. People wave flags and sing patriotic songs to the fatherland. Prominent patriots get up and give speeches telling their fellow nationals why theirs is "the greatest country in the world."

I have observed such patriotic events in scores of countries around the world. The speeches are all alike. Simply change the name of the country and the same speech can be recycled for delivery all over the planet.

If we want to celebrate together why not have a Global Day or a World Day?

Before long we will spread out across the solar system and some people will justly complain that World Day is too chauvinistic.

How Creative Are You?

1–How do you assess yourself:
  A–Innovator: create new ideas and/
    or directions? ____
  B–Refiner: improve and streamline
    others' innovations? ____
  C–Adapter: accept and go along with
    existing conditions? ____

2–Do you rely on precedence—
traditions—rules and regulations—
charters?
____Often ____Sometimes
____Hardly ever

3–Do you tend to go along with decision makers? (parents—teachers—
employers—clergy—gurus—political leaders—etc.)
____Often ____Sometimes
____Hardly ever

4–Do you take risks? For example: new
ideas—new formats—new lifestyles
—new associations—new directions.
____Often ____Sometimes
____Hardly ever

5–Does your home environment encourage questioning—cross fertilization—initiative?
____Often ____Sometimes
____Hardly ever

6–Does your work environment stimulate innovation—creativity—originality—imagination?
____Often ____Sometimes
____Hardly ever

7–How do you rate your life in the following areas:

	Rich	Moderate	Poor
A–Telecommunication?	___	___	___
B–Travels?	___	___	___
C–Leisure?	___	___	___
D–Gatherings?	___	___	___

E– Seminars?

F– Discussion groups?

—— —— ——
—— —— ——

8– How creative are you when thinking ahead?

A– A NASA official recently said that by 2035 it probably won't make sense for a woman on a lunar or Martian colony to return all the way to Earth to have a baby.

——Probably accurate
——Probably false

B– It has often been projected that by 2020 the sun-belt regions of the world will be the most populous because millions of retirees will continue to pour in from northern areas.

——Probably accurate
——Probably false

C– The World Bank recently projected that the Earth's population may double to ten billion by 2050. Most of the increase will take place in poorer countries.

——Probably accurate
——Probably false

Answer sheet: MONITOR 12

1 A _____ (2)
  B _____ (1)
  C _____

2 _____Often   _____Sometimes (1) _____Hardly ever (2)

3 _____Often   _____Sometimes (2) _____Hardly ever

4 _____Often (2)   _____Sometimes (1) _____Hardly ever

5 _____Often (2)   _____Sometimes (1) _____Hardly ever

6 _____Often (2)   _____Sometimes (1) _____Hardly ever

7

	Rich	Moderate	Poor
A	_____ (2)	_____ (1)	_____
B	_____ (2)	_____ (1)	_____
C	_____ (2)	_____ (1)	_____
D	_____ (2)	_____ (1)	_____
E	_____ (2)	_____ (1)	_____
F	_____ (2)	_____ (1)	_____

8 A _____Probably accurate (2)   _____Probably false
  B _____Probably accurate   _____Probably false (2)
  C _____Probably accurate   _____Probably false (2)

Total: _____

Who is creative?

People who generally challenge and deviate from established patterns. People who look at things in new ways.

People who do not accept limitations.

People who fantasize and allow their fantasies to materialize in the real world.

Progressives—revolutionaries—visionaries. (As a rule people who rely on precedence and traditions are not likely to be creative. They are better at implementing and interpreting.)

Scientists—inventors—designers—architects—planners—film-makers—writers—artists—composers—comedians. (Some fields demand and stimulate creativity more than others. But not everyone in the creative fields is necessarily creative. For example many scientists and architects are refiners and adapters rather than innovators. By the same token there is the potential for creativity in relatively noncreative fields. For example preparing and serving meals in new ways or acting creatively to defuse differences with people.)

What are the stimulants to creativity?

It is difficult to be precise about creativity—how much of it is inherited and how much learned. Several conditions have been shown to develop and stimulate creativity:

—An environment—particularly early home environment—that encourages free unrestricted thinking—questioning—innovating.

—An environment that encourages people to take initiatives.

—Intelligence is a variable that is necessary for creativity in some areas such as the sciences—but not as essential in other fields such as the arts.

—Updated information.

—A dynamic environment—open and ever-changing. Global telecommunication—global travel—gatherings with people of diverse backgrounds and interests—all these stimuli can light up your switch-board with new ideas.

—Leisure is indispensable to creativity. Poor regions of our world are not as a rule fertile environments for creativity mainly because everyone is locked in a struggle for survival. In more affluent societies the creative are as a rule people who enjoy a balanced ratio of leisure and fun and work. Creative scientists—writers—artists—others instinctively know the value of leisure. They do their work then go off and freefall: a walk on the beach—a drive in the countryside—a nap—a tennis game—a trip. While their system is idling ideas percolate in their heads. People who rush around or overload are rarely creative.

Why is creativity increasingly valued?

Creativity was not always highly regarded. In the past people were admired for knowing the religious books and other ancient teachings by heart. Artists as a rule prided themselves in faithfully copying and keeping alive age-old designs and imageries and music.

The oldworld valued interpreters—revivalists—adapters.

As a rule creativity and originality were viewed as heresy and discouraged. The truly creative thinkers—reformers—artists—others struggled in inhospitable climates. Many gained fame long after their deaths.

To this day most North American and European industries value employees who are content to do their work and not rock the boat. Until now this worked well because employees were not inclined to be innovative.

But things are changing. Creativity is valued more and more. For example U.S. corporations such as Kodak and IBM and government agencies have set up "offices of innovation" and "creativity workshops" to help employees develop creative skills. "Creativity training" itself is big business.

In the coming years creativity and innovation will be valued assets in all areas of telespheral life. Here are some of the reasons:

—Samuel M. Ehrenhalt—regional commissioner of the United States Bureau of Labor Statistics in New York—writes: "We are approaching a historic moment in American economic development. [By around 1990] the number of professional, managerial and technical workers will exceed the number of blue-collar workers. That will mark the end of an era that began in the early days of the 20th century, when manual workers succeeded farm workers as the most numerous group among the employed . . . While the workers of the new economy are diverse, what is common to most is the requirement for education and training, a broader latitude for creativity, independent thought and action . . . Their stock in trade is knowledge, their working tools, ideas.''[1]

—Today's young employees entering the job market are better educated and more demanding than workers in the past. These new generations grew up in reciprocal home and school environments where their opinions and initiatives were valued. They respond to consensus —not leadership. "Workers' participation movements" and "participatory management" are efforts toward workers' greater involvement in *all* areas of the work environment. These young people have high-tech attention spans and will not long put up with passive noncreative work.

—In our age of rapid recontextings ideas—policies—products— designs degrade quickly. To develop new designs and new products corporations spend billions yearly on research and development—which in turn rely on imagination and inventiveness. Government agencies also spend large sums of money setting up "brainstorming sessions" to come up with new ideas and policies for dealing with a rapidly changing world environment. Here again creativity is the most valued asset.

— Finally more and more routine work is now performed by smart machines: computers—supercomputers—expert systems—ultraintelligent systems (AI)—automated office machines—robots. These machines are getting smarter every day. In a few years they will perform most bureaucratic—managerial—secretarial—administrative—clerical functions. They will execute these tasks more efficiently and rapidly than human workers. The telespheral economy will need fewer and fewer people for repetitive noncreative jobs. The attributes that are increasingly valued are innovation—imagination—creativity.

How creative are you when thinking ahead?

Planning for the future is a creative process. You have to be well-informed in many fields and know techniques of forecasting. But you also have to be imaginative and creative.

The three questions here measure normative aspects of creativity.

Question 1. Is the NASA official accurate in his forecast that by 2035 a woman on a lunar or a Martian colony will probably not need to come back to Earth to have a baby?

This is actually an irrelevant question. A single-track.

By 2035 not only will there be large colonies of people on the moon and on Mars—a lot of other advances will have been made:

● By 2035 women will not carry babies in the womb. We will have moved beyond today's asexual insemination—embryo transfer—surrogate mothering—frozen embryos. We will have total in vitro reproduction (ectogenesis). The entire process of fertilization and gestation will take place in wholesome synthetic wombs. We may also reproduce through cloning.

● By 2035 reproduction will be totally preplanned. Computerized screening of stored sex cells will lead to cross-fertilization of the best features of different donors (mosaic births).

In 2035 therefore where anyone will be will have no bearing on reproduction.

Question 2. It has often been projected that the sun-belt regions of the world will be the most populous in 2020 because retirees from the north will keep pouring in. Is this accurate?

The answer is no.

● In 2020 we will have solar satellites. *Any* region of the planet will be able to switch on abundant sunshine. There will be no "sun belt."

● "Retirement" will be an alien concept. Rejuvenation techniques and more radical procedures will enable people to stay vigorous indefinitely.

● We will have plenty of leisure. But we will not converge on any one region of the planet. The most popular vacation places may not even be on Earth.

Question 3. Is the World Bank accurate in its projection that the Earth's population will reach ten billion in 2050 and that most of the increase will take place in "poorer countries"?

This projection has several flaws:

● In 2050 there will be an Earth population and extraterrestrial populations. Millions of people will permanently live away from this planet. Population increase will not be an issue.

● There will be no "poorer countries." In 2050 there will be no "countries"—only continental and hemispheric units. And no "poverty" because today's global economy still in its early stages will by then have matured and phased out the imbalances of wealth that exist today.

People who make projections such as the three examples given here are not familiar with the dynamics of progress. Most projections are clumsy extrapolations from *today's* conditions. They are as off target as predictions made by "authorities" decades ago. For example John Foster Dulles the U.S. secretary of state indicated in 1954 that "Japan should not expect to find a big U.S. market because the Japanese do not make the things we want."

Then there was the president of the Michigan Bank who in 1903 advised his clients not to invest in the automobile: "The horse is here to stay, but the automobile is only a novelty—a fad."

How Emotional Are You?

How much emotion (feeling) do you invest in your interactions and beliefs? For example:

	Intensely	Warmly
1–What part does "love" play in your life?		
A–How much do you love your family?	___	___
B– How much do you love your lover or spouse?	___	___
C–How much do you love your country? (how patriotic)	___	___
D– How much do you love your god? (how devout)	___	(If at all) ___
E– How much do you love your ethnic group or race?	___	___
F– How loyal are you to your political organization or party?	___Intensely	___Mildly

2–How strong are your hatreds?		
A–How many people do you actively hate in your personal life?	___Many ___None	___A few
B– How strongly do you hate certain prominent people?	___Intensely ___Not at all	___Mildly
C–How strongly do you hate members of other ideological groups (right-wingers—communists—conservatives—liberals—etc.)?	___Intensely ___Not at all	___Mildly
D–How strongly do you hate certain nationalities—races—ethnic groups (Blacks—Jews—Arabs—Russians—Latins—Germans—etc.)?	___Intensely ___Not at all	___Mildly

3–What part does anger play in your life?

A–How often are you angry at people? ____Often ____Sometimes ____Rarely

B–How often do you fight with people? ____Often ____Sometimes ____Rarely

C–How often do you "dump" your anger (from elsewhere) on your lover—spouse—family—colleagues? ____Often ____Sometimes ____Rarely

D–How often do you have major explosions? ____Often ____Sometimes ____Rarely

E–How strong is your need to punish or retaliate? ____Strong ____Mild

F–How long do you harbor anger and feelings of vengeance? ____Forever ____Long ____Brief

G–How quickly do you resolve conflicts? ____Quickly ____Slowly

4–How often are you involved in suits—litigations—disputes? ____Often ____Rarely ____Never

5–How strong are your fears? ____Very strong ____Strong ____Mild

A–Do you fear many people? ____Yes ____No

B–Do you fear certain groups (men—women—minorities—etc.)? ____Yes ____No

6–How often are you sad? ____Often ____Sometimes

A–How often do you weep? ____Often ____Sometimes ____Never

7–How often do you feel jealousy in your romances or marriage? ____Often ____Sometimes

8–How competitive are you at home—school—work—sports—politics? ____Highly ____Mildly

9–How excited do you feel watching a contest in which a person or team you are close to is involved?

_____Highly   _____Mildly

10–How quickly are your feelings hurt?

_____Very quickly_____Quickly
      _____Slowly

Answer sheet: MONITOR 13

		Intensely	Warmly	
1	A	____	____ (2)	
	B	____	____ (2)	
	C	____	____ (2)	
	D	____	____ (2) (If at all)	
	E	____	____ (2)	
	F	____Intensely	____Mildly (2)	

2	A	____Many	____A few (1)	____None (2)
	B	____Intensely	____Mildly (1)	____Not at all (2)
	C	____Intensely	____Mildly (1)	____Not at all (2)
	D	____Intensely	____Mildly	____Not at all (2)

3	A	____Often	____Sometimes (1)	____Rarely (2)
	B	____	____	____
	C	____	____	____
	D	____	____	____
	E	____Strong	____Mild (2)	
	F	____Forever	____Long	____Brief (2)
	G	____Quickly (2)	____Slowly	

4		____Often	____Rarely (1)	____Never (2)

5		____Very strong	____Strong (1)	____Mild (2)
	A	____Yes	____No (2)	
	B	____Yes	____No (2)	

6		____Often	____Sometimes (2)	
	A	____Often	____Sometimes (2)	____Never

7		____Often	____Sometimes (2)

8		____Highly	____Mildly (2)

9		____Highly	____Mildly (2)

10   ____Very quickly   ____Quickly   ____Slowly (2)

Total: _____

What are emotions?

Emotions are low-grade intelligence. Emotions are the mental and bio-chemical responses we developed in the earliest stages of our evolution to help us cope with the environment.

Emotions and intelligence are in fact part of the same continuum.

For example the emotion we call love is basically an intelligent response. We cherish love precisely because it has survival value. If love could talk it would say: "I love my mother because my very survival depends on her." In our adult lives this love is transferred to other attachment-objects such as husband or wife—lover—motherland.

There is nothing mystical or spiritual about love. Make no mistake about it—love is pragmatic—calculating—self-serving.

Vengefulness also has a rationality. If it could talk it would say: "I have to destroy this person otherwise he/she will come back and destroy me."

Throughout evolution we have valued emotions because emotions have helped us in our struggle for survival. At one time we valued bravery because brave fighters protected the tribe. We valued loyalty and possessiveness because these and other emotions helped insure the cohesiveness within our nests (family—tribe—nation).

Primitive survival emotions still dominate our lives because we are still fragile organisms. What are some of these powerful emotions? Love—hate—fear—rage—loyalty—vindictiveness—territoriality—jealousy—competitiveness.

As our societies grow more complex our survival needs change and therefore the emotions we value change also.

For example the emotions that have long helped sustain family will be less and less useful in the hyperfluid worlds ahead. Possessiveness—jealousy—sexual loyalty are steadily giving way to fluidity. Constancy and possessiveness—traditionally appreciated as evidences of a "deeply loving and feeling" person—are now increasingly perceived as indicative of insecurity and addictiveness.

Emotions that at one time led to stability now lead to pain and disruption.

At one time we admired the person who had strong convictions—who was prepared to fight and even die for them. Today we regard such people as crackpots and fanatics. We now value people who can see all sides of an issue and who are well aware that no one has a monopoly on truth—that in fact there are no absolute or eternal truths.

Then too our newly developed weapons of mass destruction have ushered in a new survival equation. Chauvinism—xenophobia—self-righteousness—competitiveness—far from protecting us in the new global environment—can now terminate us all.

We are no longer fighting with bows and arrows. We have to unlearn the habits of millions of years. Emotions that at one time had a rationale (intelligence) are now suddenly suicidal. Ethnic—racial—national loyalties have to give way to a new emotion—global loyalty.

If we attempt to repress or tamper with our emotions is there not the danger that we may turn into cold unfeeling people?

I have news for you. We are already cold and unfeeling—in the eyes of premodern people. *We* don't think of ourselves as cold and unfeeling—but this is how we are perceived by people at a less advanced stage in history.

Someone from an agrarian society (or an early twentieth-century American) observing late twentieth-century life would say:

"How cold and estranged you all are. You don't marry and settle down before you are twenty. Instead you have numerous lovers. Millions of you in your thirties and forties and fifties have never married and have no children. How is this possible? Where are your feelings?

"You don't even stay in your ancestral villages or towns. Many of you don't even remain in your homelands—where you belong. Instead you go and live far away across the world among total strangers. Where are your loyalties? How cold and impersonal late twentieth-century life is."

By the same token life in the twenty-first century may appear cold and estranged to us today. But when we arrive in the future—in a new context—we will think of ourselves as warm and friendly beings. We will look back at the final decades of the twentieth century astonished at how emotional and insecure we all were.

Is the trend then toward more or less emotion and feeling?

The evolutionary trend is toward greater intelligence.

We will continue to outgrow emotions that have no value to our evolution.

The more backward we are the more emotions dominate our lives. The more we advance the more intelligence dominates.

The more backward we are the more intense our "love" for family—spouse—lovers—leaders—gods—country. The more backward the more passionate our hatreds our anger our loyalties.

People who are highly emotional do not love better or feel more nor are they more sincere. They are just more insecure.

People who are chronically emotional make poor use of their intelligence.

We will all have survival emotions for a long time to come. Certainly for as long as we are vulnerable to pain and suffering and death. Learning to *manage* our emotions intelligently is a sure sign of an advanced person.

(More on emotions in the next monitor: Intelligence)

How Intelligent Are You?

	Often	Sometimes	Rarely

How quickly do you learn?
How often do you repeat a mistake—
after you've been corrected?
How intelligently do you manage your
emotions?
How quickly do you adapt to new and
better ways? Examples:

1–How often do you get caught in the same kind of painful romance?

2–How often do you make appointments you cannot keep or do not want to keep?

3–How often do you overload and end up angry at yourself for taking on too much?

4–How often do you take on jobs or assignments or studies that you end up not liking?

5–How often do you dead-end in projects you cannot complete because of inadequate capital or preparation?

6–How often do you interrupt people —after you have been asked to wait your turn?

7–How often do you take extra things (clothes—reading material—etc.) on trips that you end up not using at all?

8—How quickly do you jettison a romance—an association—a job that is obviously unworkable for you?

___Quickly   ___Slowly

9—How long do you go on supporting government policies that have been proven outdated and useless—simply because they satisfy (anachronistic) emotions? Examples:

A—Do you support antipornography and antinudity measures?

___Yes   ___No

B—Do you support U.S. interventions in Central America (à la Vietnam)?

___Yes   ___No

C—Do you support the death penalty?

___Yes   ___No

10—How long does it take you to cut out foods and drinks (and cigarettes) after you have been told that they are bad for you?

___Years   ___Months
___Days or weeks

11—Do you go on year after year saying that you have to get married (and have children)—though it is obvious that marriage is no longer what you *really* want or what would work for you in this new environment?

___Yes   ___No

12—How often do you fight over the same issue with the same person?

___Often   ___Rarely

13—How often do you fight over different issues with the same person?

___Often   ___Rarely

14—How often do you fight over the same issues with different people?

___Often   ___Rarely

Answer sheet: MONITOR 14

	Often	Sometimes (1)	Rarely (2)
1	———	———	———
2	———	———	———
3	———	———	———
4	———	———	———
5	———	———	———
6	———	———	———
7	———	———	———

8   ——Quickly (2) ——Slowly

9 A   ——Yes   ——No (2)
   B   ——Yes   ——No (2)
   C   ——Yes   ——No (2)

10   ——Years   ——Months   ——Days or weeks (2)

11   ——Yes   ——No (2)

12   ——Often   ——Rarely (2)

13   ——Often   ——Rarely (2)

14   ——Often   ——Rarely (2)

Total: _____

A profile of intelligence.

The questions on the self-test sheet focus on *some* of the central facets of intelligence—particularly in our fast-track world:

- The capacity to learn new information and skills quickly.
- The capacity to quickly jettison outdated information (including prejudices and old values).
- The capacity to learn from mistakes and not repeat them.
- The capacity to adapt to rapidly changing environments: new values—new technology—new lifestyles—new world situations.
- The capacity to manage emotions constructively.

All the above facets of intelligence overlap and interrelate.

Flexibility—adaptability—fluidity—creativity—spontaneity—these are *some* of the principal features of intelligence.

What are the specific tools of intelligence?

Monitoring. Intelligence is heavily influenced by the way you monitor the world around you. How subjectively or objectively you interpret things—how much information you bring to each situation and how much information you seek—how alert and tuned in you are—how effectively you see and observe and hear and listen and feel and read. Sherlock Holmes—the fictional detective—monitored the world around him intelligently and was therefore highly effective at what he did.

Knowledge base. An extensive and continually updated knowledge base is a prerequisite to intelligence and intelligent living. The more extensive and updated your knowledge base the greater your reference base and therefore the more quickly *new* information will fall into place and become integrated. When an information base is shallow or closed off new information will not find a reference base to fit in and therefore it is less likely that you will have the information-assist to act intelligently.

Information-process. As noted earlier taking in a mass of information is one thing. Processing the information is quite another. Information trickles down an elaborate sieve of personal prejudices and hardened ideas. As a rule the more *fluid* the knowledge base the better the information-process. The more granitelike the ideas you carry the poorer the processing of new information.

Feedback. People who do not actively seek feedback—in whatever they do and with whomever they interact—are disconnected and under-informed and therefore likely to act unintelligently. Ask yourself: How much feedback do I continually seek and obtain from my parents—children—lovers—spouse—students—employees—colleagues—clients—friends—others? People who only talk and seldom listen obtain very little feedback. The more questions you ask the more feedback you obtain.

Playback. How accurately do you playback events? Studies have shown that one week after exposure most people tend to remember:
—Around 10% of what they read.
—Around 20% of what they hear.
—Around 30% of what they see.
—Around 50% of what they see and hear.
Memory fade-out continues in ensuing weeks and months. Eventually very little is retained. Why?
—Memory degradation.
—Selective editing (squelching and rearranging information to suit our emotional needs).
Imagine if you had an onbody audio/visual recorder to register events (conversations—meetings—sights—etc.) for later playback and study. Your intelligence would continually benefit from a powerful assist.

Simulation. How thoroughly do you think things through? "What if I try this approach. What if I try the other approach. What if . . . What if . . ." We all automatically test out options all the time. The critical factor is how rigorously or sloppily we think things through. Because we do not carefully think ahead we often produce unintelligent results. Psychopaths are extreme examples of people who do poor simulation —never thinking ahead or considering consequences of their actions.

Error correction. Most people automatically playback a situation that went bad. But how often do you sit down to examine *exactly* what went wrong? The result: poor fault-isolation and the tendency to repeat errors.

* * *

We all deploy these component parts of our intelligence automatically. The level of intelligence depends largely on how well these processes operate individually and jointly.

Random examples of people who need to raise their level of intelligence.

The poor use of intelligence is evident in trivial matters as well as in significant issues. The tendency to act unintelligently in our interpersonal affairs is well-known. Less evident is the emotionalism and poor use of intelligence at governmental—corporate—institutional—international levels.

The public assumes that government leaders and corporate executives surrounded as they are by the paraphernalia of power act intelligently and know what they are doing.

The fact is that people in "high office" also tend to repeat mistakes—persist in the outdated and the unworkable—are slow to learn and adapt—manage their emotions poorly.

In other words they often don't know what the hell they are doing.

A case in point: government leaders in the United States—the Soviet Union—and in other aggressive nations who have not learned the lessons of recent history—that if you invade or occupy other people's territories you will pay dearly for it in many ways and in the end you will not even get away with it. One would think that people would have learned from the bloody decolonization struggles of recent decades.

Here are quick examples of poor use of intelligence in everyday matters:

People who need to be reminded over and over: "Please don't bang the car door so hard."

"It is lie down—not lay down."

"Stop calling me Marilyn. You know that I changed my name to Marla years ago."

People who participate in or support boxing though the medical profession has repeatedly warned that boxing causes irreparable damage to the brain.

Women who think of themselves as liberated yet sit passively and expect men to pay in restaurants. Or who wait for men to take initiatives and call for rendezvous.

Men who think of themselves as modern yet live by double standards expecting their wives or female lovers to be sexually "faithful" though they themselves are not.

People who oppose "pornography" and nudity offering the exact arguments given by earlier moral crusaders through the centuries in their futile efforts to preserve chastity laws—female segregation—Victorian puritanism—polygamy. You would think that today's moralists would have learned by now.

In each of the above instances—from everyday encounters to global matters—we have examples of poor use of intelligence.

Imagine the blowup of a spacecraft during liftoff. Then imagine not taking the time to study the exact causes of the malfunction but turning right around and launching a duplicate spacecraft—with the same tragic results. Then another disastrous launching and another and another.

This is how we handle most of our personal—social—economic—political—international affairs.

Exobiologists talk of looking for signs of intelligence in the universe. We should be looking for signs of intelligence right here on this planet.

How intelligently do you manage your emotions?

Emotion management is one of the hallmarks of intelligence.

How we handle our emotions is what finally distinguishes the intelligent person from the emotional—the mature from the immature—the advanced from the backward.

Intelligent people manage their emotions intelligently.

They use the tools of intelligence effectively (monitoring the environment—updated knowledge base—information-process—feedback—playback—simulation—error correction).

The intelligent use these tools automatically to create for themselves environments that deemphasize emotionalism (low intelligence) and accentuate high intelligence.

The intelligent choose their battles carefully—waging only an occasional battle that really matters and that can produce positive results.

Conflicts and disagreements in everyday matters are inevitable. How we *handle* such conflicts is a test of intelligence.

Highly emotional people fight frequently and erratically. Even small disagreements often escalate into major nuclear wars.

Emotional people fight the same battles over and over again.

Most of their battles are waged with "safe" targets: lovers— spouses—close friends—siblings—employees. Because the emotional do not monitor their environments intelligently they are often not even aware that the targets of their assaults are little more than safe garbage dumps for them.

When necessary such people deploy their intelligence effectively. For example how often do you fight with your boss?

Obviously not often. Because your intelligence tells you that if you fight with your boss you will lose your job. So you restrain yourself.

The fact that the emotional do not exercise the same restraint with people they are close to is evidence of the way they shift selectively between emotionalism (low intelligence) and high intelligence.

But why use anyone as a garbage dump? Why use people close to you as targets for terrorist attacks? Why not use your intelligence to probe the nature of your emotionalism (which may include circadian and monthly biochemical cycles) and deal with it intelligently.

The use of intelligence (including emotion management) is a valuable skill that needs to be taught.

What is the future of intelligence?

Someone once figured out that if the automobile industry had upgraded its technology at the same rate as the computer industry has we would now have Rolls-Royces selling for around $2.75 each and running a million miles to a gallon of fuel.

This is a clever analogy. But not quite on target. If the auto industry had improved its technology at the same rate as the computer sciences have it wouldn't be manufacturing automobiles at all. It would have evolved beyond the automobile—to individual vertical-lift systems. We would all now be *flying* around using jet-packs and rocket-belts and sport helicopters.

Since the 1940s automobiles have improved very little. During the same time we have evolved from room-size semimoronic computers to molecule-size whiz micro micros—agile robots—supercomputers and other ultraintelligent machines.

Suddenly something new is crystallizing in our human environment —the introduction of synthetic (electronic) intelligence.

We are learning to quantify and organize intelligence.

Every day we are creating smarter and smarter machines.

Every day these smart machines themselves go on to create smarter machines.

Every day these smart machines are incorporated into more and more areas of our environment: intelligent telephones—intelligent computers—intelligent buildings—intelligent helicopters.

Every day these smart machines and we humans are merging: intelligent prostheses—intelligent limbs—intelligent pacemakers—etc.

Electronic intelligence is still crude. But in a twenty-year period this new intelligence is racing ahead at a rate roughly equivalent to a million years in human evolution.

At this rate of growth in twenty or thirty years (around 2020) we will have ultraintelligent machines that in every way will think better than today's humans.

But we are not standing still either. As machines grow smarter we grow smarter.

We are like parents who have to continually realign simply to keep up with their smart children and smarter grandchildren.

If we people do not upgrade our intelligence—in thirty or forty years we will be obsolete. These emerging ultraintelligences may then "decide to keep us as pets" as Marvin Minsky who works in this field has noted.

I sometimes hear alarmists express the fear that intelligent machines may "take over." My main worry has been how much longer semi-intelligent people in government and in private industry will continue to make a mess of things.

The good news though is that intelligent machines are here to stay and grow and spread. Smarter and smarter machines are helping amplify our intelligence: remote monitors and scanners—instant feedback and playback mechanisms—memory reset—computer simulation—personal data bases—expert systems and other decision-assists—malfunction alert devices—collision-avoidance and fault-isolation mechanisms and much more.

The relatively intelligent environments within our spacecraft and space platforms are this very day replicated in small specialized areas of our lives here on earth. Barring an unexpected catastrophe in the coming decades we will live in increasingly intelligent environments and deal more and more intelligently with our lives.

When we speak of consciousness raising we really mean raising the level of our intelligence.

How Family Oriented Are You?

1– How much emphasis do you place on family?

____Heavy ____Mild ____None

   A– Do you love your relatives because you are related or because you value who they are as individuals?

____Because of kinship ____Who they are ____Both

   B– Among the ten *living* people you feel closest to how many are related to you?

____7–10 ____3–6 ____Under 3

   C– Do you and other *adult* relatives continue to address one another by your family titles: Mom—Dad—Son—Uncle Jack—Aunt Carol—Cousin John?

____Mostly ____Partly

   D– Do you spend major holidays with your family?

____Yes ____No

2– How important is it to you to have your own biological children—your "own flesh and blood"?

____Important
____Not important

3– What do you think of new and upcoming methods of procreation? For example:
   In vitro fertilization—frozen embryo transfer—telegenesis (fusing sex cells of people who may have never met)—ectogenesis (entire process of fertilization and gestation done out of the womb).

____Apprehensive
____Indifferent
____Enthusiastic

4– How do you feel about the fact that millions of people are voluntarily not reproducing?

____Sad ____Indifferent ____Pleased

5–Is the family as an institution declin-   ___Yes   ___No
ing?

  A–If you think that it is declining   ___Sad   ___Indifferent
how do you feel about it?   ___Pleased

6–What are *your* living arrangements?

  A–Extended family (parents—   ___
siblings—offspring—
grandparents—uncles—aunts—
cousins)

  B–Nuclear family (husband and wife   ___
and perhaps children)

  C–Coupling (two people linked in   ___
exclusive romance)

  D–Group living (shared homing with   ___
nonbiological ties)

  E–Single (emphasis on fluid net-   ___
working)

  F–Mixture of lifestyles (single/cou-   ___
pling/group living or other mix)

Answer sheet: MONITOR 15

1   ____Heavy   ____Mild (2)   ____None (1)
  A ____Because of kinship ____Who they are (2) ____Both (1)
  B ____Over 7   ____3–6 (1)   ____Under 3 (2)
  C ____Mostly   ____Partly (2)
  D ____Yes   ____No (2)

2   ____Important   ____Not important (2)

3   ____Apprehensive ____Indifferent   ____Enthusiastic (2)

4   ____Sad   ____Indifferent   ____Pleased (2)

5   ____Yes (2)   ____No
  A ____Sad   ____Indifferent   ____Pleased (2)

6 A ____
  B ____ (1)
  C ____ (1)
  D ____ (2)
  E ____ (2)
  F ____ (2)

Total: _____

How important is it to you to have your own "flesh and blood" children?

Apparently as our species advances it is less and less necessary for each of us to have children. Until a few decades ago people everywhere in the world were encouraged to have many children. The reasons for this are all well-known by now.

In recent decades the trend everywhere is toward smaller families. In fact in major cities around the planet millions of women and men are voluntarily not reproducing at all. The reasons:

● Overpopulation has lessened the pressure to reproduce.

● Focus on the quality of life. More and more women and men seek fulfillment in romances—creativity—work—personal growth.

● Parenthood is perceived (often unconsciously) as old-fashioned—expensive—time-intensive—an obstacle to glamorous global life.

Is the (nuclear) family phasing out?

The nuclear family (father—mother—children) is a relatively recent construct. Until about a hundred years ago we had clans—tribes—extended families.

Today even the nuclear family is breaking apart. Here are some quick statistics for the U.S.:

● The *traditional* nuclear family (working husband—stay-at-home wife—several children) constituted about seventy-five percent of all households in the 1950s. In the 1980s it is under seven percent. (The majority of households are now *nontraditional* formats: remarried couples—stepfamilies—childless couples—two-income homes—etc.) Also as I will indicate there is a proliferation of nonfamily options.

● Over half of all marriages end in divorce. "It's come to the point where people who get married today don't have the deadly serious attitude of till death do us part," says Dr. Robert T. London, a psychiatrist at New York University Medical Center.[1] "We want it to work, but if it breaks up, it'll break up."

● Forty-five percent of children born today can expect to live with only one parent.

● Thirty-five million Americans now live in a stepfamily unit. One of every five children is a stepchild.

- Over one of every five marriages is a remarriage. (This leads some people to assume that marriages are coming back.)
- The rate of reproduction in the United States is the lowest in its history—15.5 per 1,000 people. (The rate is even lower in several European countries.)
- The single-person household is now the fastest-growing category. One out of three adult Americans is single.
- According to the U.S. Census Bureau "the number of persons per household in the U.S. has been declining for *at least* the last one hundred years.

   In 1850 the average number of people per household was 5.55
   In 1900 it was 4.76
   In 1930   4.11
   In 1960   3.33
   In 1986   2.67"[2]

The Census Bureau projects that the average number of people per household will continue to decline.

Isn't the decline of the (nuclear) family disastrous for society?

When clans and tribes and extended families began to phase out—a more advanced format took their place—the nuclear family. In turn the nuclear family is giving way to freer more dynamic lifestyles.

It is unrealistic to think that we could have profound changes in all areas of our lives—except in our homes.

Everywhere in the world the trend is away from hereditarianism—specialization—centralization. We are moving toward voluntarism and fluidity.

For thousands of years hereditarianism was pervasive in the world. Our economic structures were hereditarian: when the father died the sons took over as landlords—farmers—soldiers—bakers. This was considered only natural.

Our political structures were also hereditarian. When the father died the son took over as tribal chief—head of clan—lord—monarch.

The last stronghold of hereditarianism is the family. Having one's own "flesh and blood" is biological territoriality.

This narcissistic specialization at the most fundamental level of life became generalized into broader self-serving territoriality (hereditarianism): tribalism—nationalism—ethnocentricity.

"My own child" and "my own parent"—all too quickly converts into "my own family"—"my own people"—"my own motherland."

To protect territory we have resorted to the most heinous aggressions against others.

Families are not only spawning grounds for territoriality. They are also too specialized. We procreate through mating. Mating in turn perpetuates the same genetic traits of the parents—over and over. The refinement of the human gene pool is therefore slow. We now have ways of accelerating this process through nonspecialized nonmating techniques.

But we have to procreate—we have to have children —how can biological hereditarianism and specialization ever phase out?

The loosening up of social ties and the development of new reproductive technologies are enabling more and more people to share not only in parenting—but also in the more basic act of procreation itself.

Tens of thousands of babies are now born every year through asexual insemination—inovulation—in vitro fertilization—adoptive pregnancies.

The words *mother—father—parents* are taking on new meanings. New methods of reproduction—"high-tech coupling" means that there are often several mothers and fathers involved in each birth: two (and soon more) genetic parents—one gestational mother—and one or two or more rearing parents.

In the coming years reproductive technologies will grow more sophisticated allowing us undreamed-of biological versatility (nonspecialization). We will have *in vitro gestation* and therefore bypass the need for even a gestational mother. The entire act of procreation from fertilization through delivery will take place outside the body.

We will also carry out "mosaic births"—combining different traits from *several* donor sperm and ova. (This is already done with cattle to produce desirable traits.) The hybrid baby will have not two but many biological parents.

These and other collaborative reproduction procedures will help us at last move beyond biological hereditarianism and specialization. "My own child'' and ''my own parents'' will have less and less meaning.

As in many insemination and adoptive births today—more and more people will not know who their biological parent or parents are. It won't matter to them. People will have many mothers and fathers.

In the coming years biological hereditarianism will be as unacceptable as political hereditarianism is today.

If the nuclear family has run its course what will replace it?

First let us remember the obvious: the more backward a society the more the emphasis on reproduction—family—marriage. The more advanced a society the less emphasis on reproduction and the shakier family and marriage.

The need to couple and bond is still strong everywhere. But the social structures within which couplings coalesce are loosening up.

Marriage still works for many people in modern societies. The *average* duration of *today's* marriage is nine years.

The nuclear family itself is taking on strange new shapes. Because of the high divorce rate there are now ex-husbands and ex-wives—ex-lovers and new lovers and ex-spouses' new mates and stepchildren and weekend children and new lovers' children and offsprings' lovers and former in-laws and other exotic offshoots.

But more and more people are turning to alternative lifestyles—often to a mix of interfaces:

- Single—exclusive or nonexclusive coupling—triads.
- Group living: shared housing—mobilias (fluid communes)—shared parenting.
- Weekend linkups—summer or winter group living—Club Med–like week-long linkup/linkouts—bicoastal and transglobal networks and romances.

How long any of these interconnections lasts does not determine its success or failure or depth of involvement.

Our social ties—in keeping with the rest of the postindustrial trajectory—are increasingly diversified and expansive.

We are learning to love in new ways—more freely more openly more creatively.

How Ecology Conscious Are You?

1–Is it true that our planet is more despoiled and polluted than ever?

_____Yes   _____No

2–Do you wish we could recapture some of the "environmental purity" of agrarian times when we lived in pastoral villages?

_____Yes   _____No

3–Are modern people increasingly estranged from nature because we live in "synthetic environments"?

_____Yes   _____No

A–Should we attempt to recapture the "oneness" it is believed we once enjoyed with nature?

_____Yes   _____No

4–Do you concur with the thesis that "small is beautiful"?

_____Yes   _____No

A–Should we redesign communities —technologies—institutions to adhere to "human scale"?

_____Yes   _____No

5–How concerned are you about problems of the environment? (For example: polluted air and polluted water)

_____Very concerned
_____Concerned _____Indifferent

6–Should we embark on extensive weather and climate modification?

_____Yes   _____No

7–Should we resort to heroic measures to save endangered species of animals?

_____Yes   _____No

8–Will the emerging postindustrial world with its heavy dependence on energy and complex technology and global traffic further damage the environment?   ___Yes   ___No

9–Are there *any* "limits to growth"?   ___Yes   ___No

Answer sheet: MONITOR 16

---

1 ____Yes   ____No (2)

2 ____Yes   ____No (2)

3 ____Yes   ____No (2)
A ____Yes   ____No (2)

4 ____Yes   ____No (2)
A ____Yes   ____No (2)

5 ____Very concerned (1)   ____Concerned (2) ____Indifferent

6 ____Yes (2)   ____No

7 ____Yes   ____No (2)

8 ____Yes   ____No (2)

9 ____Yes   ____No (2)

Total: _____

Is our planet in fact more despoiled and polluted than ever?

Our planet is not less or more polluted than in the past.

It is polluted in a different way.

For example radiation from soil—rocks—space permeated this planet in its pristine state millions of years ago. Dust pollution—volcanic ashes—forest-fire smoke were around even before the earliest primates.

Thousands of years ago the ancient Egyptians suffered from silicosis resulting from the inhalation of dust and sand. Another prevalent lung problem among ancient peoples was anthrasilicosis believed to have been caused by inhalation of carbon from oil-lamp smoke and wood fires.

Autopsies performed on the well-preserved bodies of people who lived in Alaska sometime between 1500 and 1800 revealed "pitch-black lungs filled with soot pigment" believed to have been caused by home environments heavily polluted with oil-lamp smoke.

Natural carcinogens in foods were common long before we developed pesticides. Bruce N. Ames—chairman of the biochemistry department at UC Berkeley and member of the National Academy of Sciences — recently noted that carcinogens currently found in our water supplies "are trivial relative to the background level of carcinogens in nature."[1]

In agrarian societies of recent centuries millions of people died every year of infections contracted from polluted waters. Dysentery—typhoid fever—cholera—malaria—intestinal disorders—trachoma—many other crippling and fatal diseases were widespread in "pastoral societies." These diseases still rampant in some rural areas of the world are brought on by polluted sewage systems—ponds—streams—wells.

According to United Nations studies millions of people in developing countries still haul water from distant and contaminated sources—a practice resulting in millions of deaths a year. "There was so much diarrhea, bilharzia, and cholera," a woman in Kwale—Kenya—is quoted by the *New York Times*. "Many people were dying. People didn't have time to do any other work because they were always looking for doctors to treat them. Things are better now."[2]

The United Nations Development Program and the World Bank have been introducing hand pumps and lessons in sanitation to rural communities in Africa—Asia—Latin America.

In agrarian times people washed their dirty linen and bathed and urinated in nearby streams. Hardly anyone was sensitive to the reality of "pollution." In fact the image of women blissfully washing linen at a stream has long been a metaphor for the idyllic pastoral world.

More recently we have had industrial pollution: from factories—auto emissions—nuclear power plants.

Pollution is nothing new. At no time has the environment been pure.

What is new is the concern and sensitivity about the quality of the environment.

Have we grown increasingly estranged from nature with which we were presumably in harmony at one time?

At least two fallacies underlie this assumption.

First: the myth that people in the past *felt* closer to nature because they *lived* closer to it.

Second: that our increasing ability to manage nature and subdue its excesses means that we are growing increasingly estranged from it.

The fact is that the farther back we go in history the more our ancestors were at the mercy of nature and therefore the more estranged they were from it. Nature which burned them froze them drowned them entombed them. Nature which washed away their crops and destroyed their frail habitations.

Nature was harsh arbitrary capricious.

Unable to fathom the complex causality of natural processes our ancestors anthropomorphized nature. They saw nature as a person or as gods. Through the eons a massive mythology sought to come to terms with the moods and wraths of these gods (nature). For example earthquakes—volcanic eruptions—floods were seen as punishment. "What did we do to deserve this? Why is god punishing us?"

We built cities to better protect ourselves from the ravages of nature. But a city is also nature—redesigned nature.

It is one thing to languish in an air-conditioned apartment in a city insulated from many environmental threats and talk grandly about living in "harmony with nature." It is quite another to cower in a fragile mud hut on the edge of a desert totally exposed to nature's frequent temper tantrums.

Storms—floods—earthquakes—other natural disasters exact the greatest toll in human lives in rural areas—rarely in modern cities.

People living in New York City—London—Amsterdam feel closer to nature than rural people ever could because they are less threatened by nature. They can enjoy the lovely aspects of nature without being as helplessly at its mercy.

Should we embark on extensive weather and climate modification?

Purists will of course resist such plans. Why tamper with nature? they'll say. The fact is that we have always attempted to modify nature and create safer more comfortable environments.

We need extensive weather modification to save lives. And to protect property.

Every year around the planet a couple of hundred thousand people lose their lives due to extremes of heat and cold—monsoons—floods —storms—hurricanes—tornadoes—blizzards—typhoons—tidal waves —avalanches—hailstorms—lightning . . .

Countless people are indirect victims of nasty weather: dessicated land that leaves people without food. Heavy snowfall or rainfall or cold spells that ruin crops.

We are still at the mercy of nature.

Modern technology is helping us enhance the accuracy of weather forecasts. This in itself saves many lives every year.

We have also had modest success at modifying the weather: we have increased rainfall—dispersed fog—reduced the size of hailstorms— augmented or created snow. Efforts are also under way to tame potentially devastating storms and hurricanes.

A Soviet weather expert who in 1986 helped divert snowfall from Moscow to outlying fields predicted that one day weather controllers will be able to ''create sunny days on command.''

Extensive weather and climate modification is a complex long-range project that can succeed only through international cooperation. We need supercomputers and other ultraintelligent systems that can speed-process billions of bits of information on recent and current global weather conditions and produce high-resolution simulations of climate change and its impact on all areas of life.

The task is awesome. But then today's global weather service would have seemed awesome to the world of thirty years ago.

Early in the twenty-first century we will choreograph weather conditions over a *given region* with the ease with which we currently control the temperature in a vast shopping mall or a giant domed stadium.

''Next week we have a five-day holiday and the Department of Climate Regulation has promised five days of blue skies and sunshine.''

Should we attempt to save endangered species of animals?

Paleontologists estimate that over 99.99 percent of all the species that have ever existed on this planet have become extinct. Most of these species disappeared long before we humans appeared on the scene.

We are wasting time and resources attempting to save endangered species. I do not condone hunting and fishing. But these species will die out anyway because they are losing viability in an ever-changing ecological equation. For one thing their habitats are shrinking.

Ironically the people who support efforts to save endangered species are often the ones most opposed to human "tamperings" with nature. But the attempt to save dying species is itself a meddling in the ways of nature.

I have another reservation. Many of the species on everyone's endangered list are predators: lions—tigers—leopards—panthers—wolves—perhaps hyenas and others. Has anybody taken a poll among gazelles and wildebeasts and zebras and all other prey of predators to learn how *they* feel about efforts to save their deadly enemies—the carnivores?

Has anybody consulted villagers in Africa and in India to learn how *they* feel about predators that terrorize and mangle and devour them and their cattle?

Why don't we *try* to change the eating habits of some carnivores? Pet dogs and cats have been weaned away from dead flesh and have thrived. Why not try the same thing with other animals? We have retrained the most ferocious and humorless predators to live among people and small animals without making a meal of anyone.

I realize that this would be a massive undertaking and in the end may change the menus of only a few of the large carnivores. Still this may prove a less difficult task than trying to save them.

What about the "balance of nature"?

Why not call it what it is—the balance of violence?

We should want to create a new balance—free of violence and terror—free of the survival imperative of the strong preying on the weak.

If animals tear one another to pieces to maintain some arbitrary "balance of nature" I say to hell with such a violent balance. Who says we need such a balance? Why not invest our genius to create a planet relatively free of predation and violence?

Will the emerging postindustrial world with its heavy dependence on energy and complex technology and global traffic further despoil the environment?

The telespheral age will be friendly to the environment—certainly far friendlier than were the agrarian and industrial ages. Here are some of the reasons:

• In the new age we will move beyond polluting fossil fuels to new sources of energy: solar power—nuclear fusion (not fission)—geothermal energy—hydrogen fuel—others. These sources of energy are clean—inexpensive and virtually inexhaustible.

• We are shifting from heavy industry (for example steel) to light industry (electronics).

• Many production units will float on the ocean and in earth orbit. They will not damage the countryside or the oceans and will not hog any space in or around our communities.

• Computerized telefarming and total-environment (microclimate) food growing will significantly reduce the need for pesticides and toxic chemicals.

• New transportation systems such as hypersonic spaceplanes will use nonpolluting hydrogen fuel or laser power or microwave. Short-range vehicles such as helicopters—short-take-off-and-landing—hovercrafts—etc.—may be powered by solar energy.

• Ultraintelligent machines with the support of remote sensors—geophones—sniffers will continually monitor the environment—both local and global. We will have a clearer understanding of the cause and effect of pollutants in the atmosphere—the dynamics of the ozone level—and other unresolved issues such as whether the garbage we dump into the oceans every day pollutes our waters or is appreciatively consumed by marine life.

We are at the beginning of all this. The telespheral age will steadily unfold in the coming years.

It is encouraging that more and more people are growing aware of ecology and clamor for cleaner air and water—greater vigilance over the use of toxic chemicals in food—stricter supervision of nuclear power plants—intelligent planning for community growth—protection of coastal regions and so on.

Scientists from many disciplines and from all over the planet recently created a Global Ecology Research Agency for a long-range focus on "global habitability."

We need an enlightened approach to ecology. But our vigilance should not be subverted into a pretext to slow down growth. We need growth—a new kind of growth—beyond the feudal and the industrial.

Is small beautiful? Should we design systems based on "human scales"?

What is "human scale"? Our scales are continually changing. At one time a small village was considered the ideal size. Today tens of millions of people living in cities consider a feudal village too confining. Urban dwellers may not know their neighbors—but they have a large network of intimate friends and associates all over the city.

In the postindustrial age the scales are widening even more. A large city may no longer be the right human scale. People are spreading out creating intimate networks across an entire region—country—continent.

In our global age the size of a community (or organization) no longer determines the level of intimacy or effectiveness.

One day we will find our very planet too confining. The entire biosphere will not be the right "human scale" to match our expanding activities and visions.

Small is *not* beautiful. Exhorting people to think and plan small is antifuture. There is nothing small about our dynamic species. We are forever growing—spreading out farther and farther—opening up ever larger environments that in turn enlarge us.

We are a dynamic species precisely because we have vision. We dare to think Big.

Are there any "limits to growth"?

What limits? The only limits are in some people's imaginations.

How ridiculous to talk of limits at this very moment in evolution when we are expanding into a limitless universe of limitless resources—limitless space—limitless time—limitless potentials—limitless growth.

How Telecommunitized Are You?

1–Do you live in a high-density–industrialized city? (For example: New York—Chicago —London—Paris—Hamburg)   ____Yes   ____No

2–Are you disoriented in a low-density–de-centralized metropolis—one that has no substantial downtown—only satellite communities loosely held together? (For example: Los Angeles—San Diego—Houston)   ____Yes   ____No

3–Do you live in a small rural town—or on a farm—far away from a city?   ____Yes   ____No

4–Do you live in a resort community? (For example: East Hampton—Palm Beach— Negril Beach—Puerto Vallarta—Palm Springs—Laguna Beach—Carmel— Pataya—Cannes)   ____Yes   ____No

5–Do you actually translive in two or more places—cities *and* resorts? For example:
- New York/Southampton/Washington, D.C.
- San Francisco/Mill Valley/Monterey/Maui
- Munich/Gstaad/Positano/Torremolinos
   ____Yes   ____No

6–Do you live in a perpetual electronic community—a telecommunity? In other words are you so intensively teleconnected that it does not matter where you are—you are always in-community?   ____Yes   ____No

Answer sheet: MONITOR 17

1 ____Yes (1)   ____No (2)

2 ____Yes   ____No (2)

3 ____Yes   ____No (2)

4 ____Yes (2)   ____No

5 ____Yes (2)   ____No

6 ____Yes (2)   ____No

Total: _____

Cities: high—and low—density.

For hundreds of years towns and cities were centers of commerce and culture and political power. Trends started here and spread to rural areas.

In our times cities still wield much influence. Many of the forces of progress crystallize here. But major cities are no longer *centers* of influence and power.

There are no centers any longer. Global telecommunication—global mobility—global economics are helping decentralize influence and wealth.

The forces of change now coalesce in many places. Resort towns and Club Meds and Disney Worlds and world fairs and film festivals—wherever large numbers of the upwardly updated interconnect. Airport communities are also powerful generators of ideas: hundreds of thousands of people convene here every day for conventions and conferences.

The fact that many of these instant communities are hyperfluid and no more than quick linkup/linkouts does not diminish their impact.

New ideas and directions are also generated in other ways—via electronic telecommunities. People connecting not in person but cross-fertilizing via hookups.

Meanwhile major transformations are unfolding within cities. The cities themselves are decentralizing. They are spreading out.

To people living in California or Arizona the old cities of the East Coast and of Europe—with their narrow dark alleys and congested streets and massive stone buildings—appear old and yestercentury. These eighteenth- and nineteenth-century cities loom like giant movie sets.

By the same token to many residents of New York and Boston and Vienna the new spread-out communities of the West Coast appear sterile and alienating.

This is exactly what rural America and Europe of the nineteenth century thought of the emerging industrial-age cities.

The fact is that it is difficult to make a rapid transition to the postindustrial world while still living in old cities.

Resort communities.

These communities though small do not suffer from the privations and isolation of traditional small towns. Quite the contrary most resort towns are alive and worldly.

People linkup from all parts of the planet. The flow of people is constant. The emphasis is on fun and relaxation.

The communication revolution is enabling more and more people to conduct their business from these resort getaways—often from poolside and beach.

More and more resort towns are coming on line. They are now everywhere: in Hawaii—Mexico—California—Arizona—Florida—Long Island—Connecticut—the Caribbean—the French and Italian Rivieras—the Costa del Sol—all over Africa and Asia.

Resort towns are evolving into powerful trendsetters—exerting influence beyond their modest sizes.

More than the big cities these hedonistic communities languishing in wholesome settings capture the esthetics and rhythms of the coming decades.

Transliving in several places.

If you live in only one place—however dynamic the community—lethargy and redundancy set in. You fall into noncreative psychological—social—intellectual grooves.

It is no longer only the wealthy who translive in several communities. Millions of middle-income people are mobile as never before. They may have a principal base in a city and *share* weekend or summer/winter homes in the country.

At present the forwardly mobile have linkup places only within a region or a country—perhaps a continent. In a few years' hypersonic aircraft will enable people to translive all over the planet.

"Where do you live?"

"I live in Stockholm—Capri—San Diego—Kyoto—Sydney—BA."

"Where do *you* live?"

"I live in Nairobi—Marrakesh—Saint Tropez—KL—Bali—Montreal—Punta del Este—Aruba."

The whole planet will be a liftoff/landing platform.

We will all be within one or two hypersonic hours of *anywhere* on the planet.

I am aware that there are people *today* who translive all over the world. But they are the exceptions—the liberated rich. By the turn of the century millions of middle-income people will share homes all over the planet.

Telecommunity—and the teleglobal life.

People who are intensively teleconnected live in a "perpetual community"—a teleglobal community. Such people flow in telecommunication-intensive environments that comprise telephones—picturephones (videophones)—TV sets—radios—computers—audio/visuals—answering machines—locators—automatic call forwarding—go-anywhere transceivers.

They have two-way telecom wherever they are—in their homes—offices—runaway retreats—cars—airplanes. And above all on their bodies.

They are at all times hooked up. They can reach out across the planet from wherever they are. And they can be reached wherever they are.

They live in a continuous electronic community. They are always in-community—no matter where they are.

"Hi Peter—this is Sylvana. Do you want to rendezvous this afternoon in Santa Monica for a walk on the beach?"

"I can't this afternoon. Right now I am in Amizmiz—North Africa. I am flying to Bermuda tonight and will be back in L.A. on Wednesday. How about linkup Wednesday evening?"

What if you want privacy? What if you want to drop out and do not want to be disturbed? Simple. Just disconnect your onbody interactives. Click click—you have disorbited. You cannot be disturbed. Click click—you are back in-community.

People who translive in a perpetual teleglobal community are the wave of the future.

"Where do you live?"

"I live everywhere."

How Global Are You?

1–Are you patriotic—attached to your country? For example: ___Strongly ___Mildly ___Not at all

  A–Do you always stick up for your country in international disputes—"my country right or wrong"?   ___Yes ___No

  B–Are you offended or embarrassed when your country is criticized by others?   ___Yes ___No

  C–Do you feel proud when your country outshines others in some endeavor?   ___Yes ___No

  D–How do you feel when your national anthem is played?   ___Inspired ___Indifferent ___Offended

2–Is nationalism in our times a progressive or a reactionary force?   ___Progressive ___Reactionary

3–Do you like the fact that we have many languages in the world? Would you rather we had one global language?   ___Many languages ___Global language

4–How should we deal with the issue of "illegal aliens"?   ___Harshly ___Tolerantly ___Do away with borders

5–What do you think of "intrusions into internal affairs of other nations"?   ___Opposed to all intrusions ___Supportive if not forced

6–What do you think of the United Nations?   ___Supportive ___Opposed

7–What do you think of transnational corporations?   ___Supportive ___Opposed

8–Will a world *without* nations lead to global sameness (homogeneity)?   ___Yes   ___No

9–How updated are you on global affairs?
A– How many countries in the EEC?   ___
B– What is ASEAN?   ___
C– COMCON?   ___
D– WHO—ILO—FAO are specialized agencies of what organization?   ___

10–How transglobal is your own environment? For example:
A– Do you have a global network of friends?   ___Yes   ___No
B– Do you teleconference or videoconference globally?   ___Often   ___Sometimes
___Never
C– Do you see films and TV programs from other countries?   ___Often   ___Sometimes
___Never
D– Do you read global and/or "foreign" newspapers and magazines?   ___Yes   ___No
E– Do you go on global travels?   ___Often   ___Sometimes
___Never
F– Are you affiliated with any international organizations?   ___Yes   ___No

Answer sheet: MONITOR 18

1 ____Strongly   ____Mildly (1)   ____Not at all (2)
- **A** ____Yes   ____No (2)
- **B** ____Yes   ____No (2)
- **C** ____Yes   ____No (2)
- **D** ____Inspired   ____Indifferent (2)   ____Offended (1)

2 ____Progressive   ____Reactionary (2)

3 ____Many languages (1)   ____Global language (2)

4 ____Harshly   ____Tolerantly (1)   ____Do away with borders (2)

5 ____Opposed to all intrusions
____Supportive if not forced (2)

6 ____Supportive (2) ____Opposed

7 ____Supportive (2) ____Opposed

8 ____Yes   ____No (2)

9 A 12 (2)
- **B** Association of Southeast Asian Nations (2)
- **C** East European Common Market (2)
- **D** United Nations (2)

10 A ____Yes (2)   ____No
- **B** ____Often (2)   ____Sometimes (1) ____Never
- **C** ____Often (2)   ____Sometimes (1) ____Never
- **D** ____Yes (2)   ____No
- **E** ____Often (2)   ____Sometimes (1) ____Never
- **F** ____Yes (2)   ____No

Total: _____

Is nationalism in our times a progressive or a reactionary force?

During the colonial era nationalism was a progressive movement that sought to do away with hegemony—the domination of one people by another.

The decolonization struggles of the late 1940s the 1950s and the 1960s have very nearly freed the world of colonies. Today there are only a handful of occupied territories in the world. In these areas only nationalism remains a necessary revolutionary force.

Everywhere else in the world nationalism is now a reactionary movement that perpetuates the divisive fragmentation of humanity.

In the age of regional groupings—common markets—global corporations—a global financial market—global telecommunication the nation state is an anachronism. It is an anachronism with distinct disadvantages.

As the members of the West European Common Market (EEC) have learned the surest way a nation can grow economically and assert political influence in today's world is through integration with neighboring states.

The EEC which in the late 1950s and the 1960s was laughed at as unworkable—is now a powerful economic and political entity moving toward ever-closer integration.

There are other such integrationist movements all over the planet. COMCON in Eastern Europe. The 22-nation Arab Common Market. The 14-nation West African group. The Southeast Asian group called ASEAN. The fledgling South Pacific Common Market—comprising Australia—New Zealand—several nearby islands. The Andean Group made up of five South American nations.

Even the United States—Canada—Mexico are this very day locked together in countless economic and regional interconnections from which none of the three can any longer disengage.

The degree of success of regional groupings varies. But the fact is that there is a persistent trend everywhere to break out of the limitations of the nation state.

Subcontinentalism—continentalism—globalization—these are the progressive movements of our times. They run concurrently reinforcing one another.

What about the apparent rise of nationalism all over the world?

If patriotism appears to be on the rise in many parts of the world it is mainly because the rampage of globalism is threatening national identities as never before.

Take the United States of America for an example. This country today is flooded as never in the past by an ever-expanding stream of immigrants—tourists—outside investors—exchange students—"illegal aliens."

The U.S. market is flooded by an avalanche of imports from all over the world. Toyotas—Hondas—Volvos—Sonys—Siemenses—croissants—quiches—falafels—Perriers—etc.

The quintessential American dream machine—the automobile—no longer exists. The Detroit car is now a multinational hybrid comprised of parts from Japan and Korea and Germany and France.

More and more U.S. banks—industries—newspapers—TV stations—film studios—book publishers are now owned or co-owned by outsiders: Venezuelans—Saudi Arabians—Kuwaitis—Iranians—Israelis—English—Germans—Australians—Japanese—others.

These investors exert powerful influences in all areas of American life.

Go through any major American city today and you will find that entire neighborhoods have been taken over by recent arrivals: Mexicans—Central Americans—Cubans—Jamaicans—Vietnamese—Cambodians—Thais—Koreans . . .

"Whose America Is It Anyway?" and "Is America Becoming a Foreign Country?"—these titles of recent TV network programs are recurrent questions on many people's minds.

Several states have considered passing laws to declare *English* the official language of the U.S.!

American patriotism is chiefly an attempt to compensate for the steady blurring of national identity and the diminution of the *relative* power and influence of the United States in an increasingly assertive world.

Gloatings of some Americans over being "number one" in the world—for example in an international sports arena—are evidence—not of national confidence—but compensations for loss of national self-esteem.

This global incursion is going on everywhere. "Will We Still Be French in Thirty Years?" a recent French TV program wondered as more and more Africans and Asians and fellow Europeans pour into that country.

Israelis wonder out loud if their country will "still be a Jewish state in thirty years." Meanwhile more and more Jews leave to settle elsewhere and Arabs proliferate all around them.

Nearby in Arab countries Moslem fundamentalists rail against "Western influences" that they believe dilute their national and religious identities.

In the 1950s and the 1960s alarmists the world over worried about the alleged "Americanization of the world." Today American alarmists worry about the "Latinization of America." Others worry about the "Orientalization of America."

The fact is that the world is not being Americanized or Latinized or Orientalized or Europeanized or Sovietized. We are all being globalized.

For the first time the forces of global integration are gaining over age-old territoriality and segregation.

As we all steadily outgrow the tribal programmings of millenniums and develop global instincts and institutions patriots everywhere will grow more strident.

There is much talk these days about the decline of America and American industry. How correct is this?

The U.S. is not declining. Other parts of the world are surging.

The global spread of wealth and information and technology is rapidly redressing imbalances in the world.

But the new giants will not be other nations—not Japan or China or the Soviet Union or Brazil. The new giants will be continental and global entities: continental common markets—global electronic markets—global corporations—multinational mergers.

In the 1950s and the 1960s Europeans and Asians and others had to be reassured that the United States was not taking over the world. In the 1980s and the 1990s Americans have to be reassured that the world is not taking over the United States.

The loss of American markets to others and the takeover of American industries by non-Americans is part of a globalization process now gaining momentum. Everything that leaves the United States (or any country) will sooner or later come back.

"Illegal aliens."

There are no illegal aliens—only illegal borders.

If it is wrong to bar people from leaving their countries it is also wrong to disallow people from coming into countries.

The issue of "illegal aliens" is a complex global matter and it will not go away by simply attempting to seal borders.

1—As more and more nations are finding out it is now impossible to stop people from sneaking across borders. In the age of helicopters —small private aircraft—motorboats—mass travel—borders have lost meaning. You can spend millions to shut down your borders—people will still come in.

2—Americans and some Europeans are under the mistaken impression that if they "opened the gates" the whole world would come rushing in. It is true that the U.S. and most European nations offer many economic and social opportunities. But they are not *everybody's* idea of paradise. There are tens of millions of "illegal aliens" all over the world. No one knows the exact numbers. They are everywhere: in Canada—Mexico—Costa Rica—Venezuela—Colombia—Brazil— Kenya—Nigeria—Ghana—Algeria—Libya—Tunisia—Saudi Arabia —Kuwait—United Arab Emirates—Greece—Pakistan—Thailand— New Zealand—Australia.

A few years ago a poll was taken around the world to find out people's preferences of countries to emigrate to if the need arose. Canada— Australia—New Zealand—Sweden—Brazil were the favorites.

3—Freedom of movement is or ought to be a basic freedom. This is *our* planet. We should have the right to go anywhere we please. National frontiers are nothing more than pissing borders charted by dogs. "This is *my* territory because I peed here first."

The millions of dollars currently dissipated by many nations in futile attempts to stop the flow of "illegal aliens" should be rechanneled to help raise everybody's living standards so that people will travel not because of economic or political pressures but to spread out and grow.

We do not want secure borders. We do not even want open borders. We want no borders.

If governments do not do away with borders—modern technology will.

The myth of "internal affairs" of nations.

There are no "internal affairs" of nations any longer.

Nonintervention in internal affairs is no longer possible—or even desirable.

All nations want more tourists—more outside investors—more exchange students and teachers and scientists—more global publications and global TV and radio—more joint manufacture—more trade.

It is ridiculous to want all these and still insist on nonintervention.

Then too in the age of nuclear power plants—weather modification —global resource interdependence—direct satellite broadcast—global corporations we *are* already involved in one another's internal affairs.

A nuclear plant malfunction such as the Chernobyl debacle can send radioactive material around the world. Weather modification in the U.S. has affected weather conditions in Canada. The price of oil in Saudi Arabia and Iran has sent economic shock waves all over the world. National elections in the United States and leadership struggles in the Soviet Union are concerns of *all* peoples because the results affect the whole planet.

In a world daily growing more interinvolved it is downright hypocritical to even pretend that there are—or ought to be—"internal affairs."

We want more and more involvement in one another's affairs. Not less. Anything happening anywhere is the affair of the entire global community.

It is understood that we do not want military or other aggressive encroachments—but positive involvement.

140

What about the United Nations?

"If there were no United Nations"—someone once observed—"the world would be scrambling to create one."

For hundreds of years people have wished for a world government. Now at last we have the beginnings of one.

The United Nations has at times been ineffective in resolving disputes only because this world organization is comprised of around 160 nations each with its own vested interests. The U.N. struggles in a world whose habits are still largely territorial and tribal. The fact that the U.N. has endured since its inception in the mid-1940s is a triumph.

As we all outgrow the tribal/national habits of thousands of years and learn to interact globally the United Nations will evolve into a truly world organization.

Meanwhile the U.N. through its subsidiary agencies quietly goes about distributing food to the impoverished of the world—fighting disease and ignorance and overpopulation—arbitrating feuds—helping improve techniques of food production—sponsoring global conferences on the peaceful uses of the ocean floor and space. . . .

The United Nations represents the best that is in each of us.

Transnational corporations.

"The only thing worse than having a transnational corporation is *not* having one." Whoever said this was certainly on target. So long as we have corporations I would rather they were transnational.

Corporations (like everything else) are spilling over national borders in their efforts to grow and make profits. They help the globalization process by spreading capital and merchandise and modern manufacturing techniques and modern managerial practices all over the world.

Will a world without nations lead to global sameness?

This common concern issues from a faulty premise—that diversity should be based on nationality and ethnicity. The fact is that a world of nations is a world of national homogeneities.

Eight million Saudi Arabians sound and dress alike. Where is the diversity in that?

Several million Bolivians have distinctly similar lifestyles and characteristics. Where is the diversity?

Tens of millions of Chinese sound and dress and live more or less alike. Is this diversity?

Is this what we want to perpetuate?

Nationality compels mass conformity to a national image. Inevitably a national profile—a certain sameness—congeals. All Bulgarians—all Guatemalans—all Laotians have distinct national traits.

Until recently people within most nations all dressed alike—thought alike—had the same fears and hopes and prejudices—ate the same foods—enjoyed the same music—observed the same holidays—worshiped the same gods. They even looked alike.

In fact the more distinctive the national or ethnic "purity" the more predictable the sameness of the people. Visit a slow backwater community anywhere in the world and within just a few days you will be able to predict everyone's reactions and moves.

Globalization is helping blur these rigid blocs of national sameness enabling each individual to respond in its own way to the crosscurrent of world influences.

It is when the Ethiopian or Hungarian or Chinese leaves his or her homeland and lives among other peoples that she or he mutates into an interesting individualistic hybrid.

It is increasingly difficult to identify the origins of the forwardly mobile of the world.

National and ethnic crossovers will accelerate diversity. Certainly for many years to come.

But by around the year 2020 diversity may come full circle and give way to global uniformity. However we need not worry about that.

By the beginning of the new century we will be well on our way to outgrowing the planet itself. We will spread out across the solar system.

Globalism is not a final destination. Only a momentum swing to yet larger worlds.

What is your nationality?

Where are you from? Where were you born? Where are your parents from? What passport do you carry?

Responses to such questions no longer define who you are or how you perceive yourself.

In our times questions about nationality make less and less sense. A more appropriate question is: "Where do you currently reside?"

This may not satisfy people who still resort to old cataloging habits. "But what is your nationality?" they will insist. "Where are you from?"

More and more people are now apt to respond: "I am from planet Earth. I have lived in many parts of the world. I feel at home in many places. I have a global network of friends and ties. I am plugged into global telecommunication. I feel involved in the joys and the sorrows of people everywhere. I am a global person."

How Cosmic Are You?

1–Do you think the U.S. spends too much or too little on the Space program?

____Too much ____Too little ____About right

2–Should we attend to pressing problems here on Earth before venturing into Space?

____Yes ____No

3–What do you think of permanent colonies in Earth orbit—on the moon —on Mars—in deep Space?

____Very supportive
____Supportive
____Opposed

4–Would you like to travel out of our planet one day soon?

____No ____Can't wait

5–How do you view our extension into Space?

____Historic ____Evolutionary
____No big deal

6–What impact will our presence in Space have on our situation here on Earth in the coming years?

____Mild impact
____Profound impact

7–What do you think of our current efforts to search for extraterrestrials?
A–Would we suffer or benefit from such contacts?
B– What do you think of UFOs (unidentified flying objects)?

____Supportive ____Opposed

____Probably suffer
____Probably benefit
____Real ____Fiction
____Not sure

8–How often do you go to planetariums and observatories?

____Often ____Sometimes
____Never

9–Are you a member of any Space-related organization?

____Yes ____No

10–Do you subscribe to a publication that focuses on astronomy—Space sciences—astrophysics—cosmology?   ____Yes   ____No

    A–Or a general science publication that regularly reports on these fields?   ____Yes   ____No

11–How informed are you about our new extraterrestrial environment?

    A–Where is Space?   _____

    B–Some scientists speak of "industrializing Space." Is this possible?   ____Yes   ____No

    C–When is the next time we will see Halley's Comet?   ____2018   ____2061   ____Depends

    D–Has any spacecraft of ours ever left the solar system?   ____Yes   ____No

    E–What are Phobos and Deimos?   _____

    F–What is a supernova?   _____

    G–When you look out into Space (at night) what are you looking at?   ____Past   ____Present   ____Future

    H–Roughly how far apart are stars in our part of the Milky Way?   _____

Answer sheet: MONITOR 19

1 ____Too much   ____Too little (2)   ____About right

2 ____Yes   ____No (2)

3 ____Very Supportive (2)   ____Supportive   ____Opposed

4 ____No   ____Can't wait (2)

5 ____Historic   ____Evolutionary (2)   ____No big deal

6 ____Mild impact   ____Profound impact (2)

7 ____Supportive (2) ____Opposed
  A ____Probably suffer____Probably benefit (2)
  B ____Real   ____Fiction (2)   ____Not sure (1)

8 ____Often (2)   ____Sometimes (1)   ____Never

9 ____Yes (2)   ____No

10 ____Yes (2)   ____No
  A ____Yes (2)   ____No

11A Everything beyond Earth's atmosphere (2)
  B ____Yes   ____No (2)
  C ____2018   ____2061 (1)   ____Depends (2)
  D ____Yes (2)—(Pioneer 10)
  E The tiny moons of Mars (2)
  F Explosion of a star (2)
  G ____Past (2)   ____Present (2)   ____Future (2)
  H Around 4 light years (2)

Total: _____

(Explanation of answers)

11B– Industrializing Space? Fossil fuels and mechanical technology did not launch us into Space and will not sustain us in new worlds. Do we want smokestacks and automobiles in Space colonies?

11C– Next time we see Halley's Comet? People on Earth will see it again in 2061. But long before then millions of us will have spread out across the solar system and beyond and may therefore see Halley's Comet at different times.

11G– What do you see when you look out into Space? The *past* because some of the tired light that reaches us comes from stars that no longer exist. The present because we can see planets—moons—stars in real time (they are there now). The *future* because some of the cosmic gases and swirls are this very day in the process of crystallizing into stars.

Are we spending too much on the Space program? Should we not attend to pressing problems here on Earth before venturing into Space?

Such objections to the Space program were frequently heard in the 1960s and the 1970s. As the benefits of our Space ventures have become more obvious such reservations—though still heard—have lost some of their ferocity.

In reaching out into Space we are in fact attending to pressing problems right here on Earth.

We long-range planners would like to see *more* funds allocated to the Space program because we believe that such an emphasis will accelerate the pace of progress in every area of human life.

We all need to be well-informed about Space because Space is our new frontier. Space will be the pivotal transformer of conditions on this planet in the decades to come.

We can no longer work out social—economic—international plans without factoring in the Space imperative.

Though in its infancy the Space program has already revolutionized

such fields as telecommunication—weather and climate forecasting—
environmental research—mapping and charting—agriculture—geology
—metallurgy—oceanography—resource exploration—others.

For example communication satellites have ushered in global
television—direct-dial global telephone—electronic mail—two-way
teleducation (for instance for hundreds of previously blacked-out villages in India and Alaska and elsewhere).

Environmental satellites continually monitor the quality of air and
water—measure concentrations of pollutants in the Earth's atmosphere—give early warnings of forest fires and hurricanes and storms
and volcanic eruptions.

Land-surveying satellites using remote-sensing locate the presence of
subsurface water resources—minerals—fuels. In fact thanks to these
satellites we now know that the Earth contains vast amounts of subsurface water supplies and that we are currently drawing from only
about one hundredth of one percent of the total world supply of fresh
water.

Thanks also to remote-sensing we have found hundreds of locations
all over the planet rich in oil—coal—minerals such as copper and iron.

Satellites help in countless other ways: identifying crops for more
accurate forecasts of harvests—helping plan the growth of urban
communities—helping climatologists improve techniques for predicting
long-term climatic patterns—helping monitor worldwide compliance
with arms control agreements and so on.

The Space program has also helped us develop an endless variety of
hardware: construction material—home appliances—transportation systems—solar energy units—clothing materials—medical technology.

Our new Space environment already plays a significant part in the
global economy. In the coming years it will play a *central* role in the
emerging social—economic—international spheres.

Before the Space age we were confined to a finite world of finite
resources—finite space—finite growth. The Space breakthrough has in
one sweep forever done away with our finiteness.

Suddenly we find ourselves in a new environment of limitless
space—limitless energy—limitless raw materials—limitless food—
limitless growth.

We have enough resources enough space enough opportunities for
growth to last us for millions of years—for billions of years. Enough
to last us for as long as there is a universe.

What impact has the Space breakthrough had on our consciousness?

Our breakout into Space has forever altered our perceptions of ourselves. We are acquiring a global and cosmic consciousness. We are just not aware of it.

In the mid-1960s at a seminar on future studies at the New School for Social Research in New York City I asked how the participants felt about the Space program and if they had any desires to travel out of this world one day. (In those early years of the Space age even in our futurist seminars there was resistance to the Space program.)

"I know that you will think I am old-fashioned—" a woman spoke up. "But the fact is that I don't want to go into Space. I love our world. I am perfectly happy here."

"Do you realize what you are saying?" I responded. "You are thinking like a global person. You express attachment to this *entire* planet. This in itself is revolutionary—even visionary. Yet you are afraid you might be perceived as old-fashioned. Before the Space age few ever related to the whole world. People expressed attachment to their tribes and homelands."

Sultan al Saud an Arab Space traveler who orbited our planet with American and French crewmates in the mid-1980s said on his return to Earth:

> On the first and second day of the flight, we all noticed our countries—"That's my home" we each said. By the third day you only see continents. By the fifth day you see only Earth—it becomes one place—your home. It is an amazing feeling.

No less amazing is the fact that this Saudi Space visitor probably grew up in a tribal community. Then a massive leap to a one-world and the solar system.

The radical conceptual shift that he and astronauts of other nations go through in a few days—the rest of humanity is going through in a few years.

Is Space exploration a historic event—an evolutionary turning point—or is it no big deal at all?

Our breakout from this planet is an evolutionary event. A major perturbation. Make no mistake about it.

We are Earth-spawned organisms—products of specific conditions on this specific biosphere. We have suddenly decoupled from our natural habitat. The consequences are beyond our current frameworks of reference.

Elsewhere in the solar system environmental conditions are radically different from Earth-normal. Different periodicities of light and darkness—different atmospheres or no atmospheres—different temperatures and climate variables—different gravities and distances from the sun—different geological and topographic configurations.

In time these new worlds away from our natural habitat will transform us in fundamental ways. We cannot indefinitely live and travel across the solar system and beyond with these Earth-specific bodies—brains —senses—speech communicaton—bipedal locomotion.

To find an event that approximates the magnitude of this twentieth-century breakaway from our planet we would have to switch back— not hundreds of years or thousands or even a few million years. We would have to go back several hundred million years when the earliest life forms migrated from the oceans to land.

We are still at the very beginning of our emergence into a new environment and therefore cannot appreciate its long-term significance.

What about permanent extraterrestrial colonies?

We have already launched small Space colonies: Salyut—Skylab— Mir. People have lived in these modest Earth-orbiting platforms for months at a time.

In the coming years more ambitious Space colonies will proliferate. The more such habitats we launch the quicker the pace of progress here on Earth.

I am not sympathetic to the scenarios of some Space scientists who would have us replicate "Earth-like conditions" elsewhere in the solar system. Eight-to-five jobs in offices and farms—"housewives" in two-story houses—children studying in schools—banks—retail stores—slaughterhouses—small towns—national enclaves—etc.

Such low-resolution scenarios sound like nostalgic playbacks of some Space scientist's childhood days in Kansas or Idaho—in the 1940s.

Do we want to undertake the gigantic expense and effort of traveling long distances simply to re-create what we have here? Do we want to start off in new worlds perpetuating "Earth-like conditions" that for eons have brought human suffering—greed—misery—conflicts?

Extraterrestrial communities offer unique opportunities for fresh starts in all areas of life.

(For details please see Monitor 20: Ideology. Also please see the books *Up-Wingers* and *Telespheres*.)

The search for extraterrestrials.

It is estimated that there are billions of galaxies in the universe each containing hundreds of billions of stars. Many of these stars have planetary systems in which life forms may have coalesced.

Our universe may be teeming with intelligent life—some less advanced than we others more advanced.

The U.S.—the Soviet Union—other nations have embarked on systematic efforts to search for intelligences in the universe. Some of these efforts are collaborative—involving scientists all over the planet.

One of the most ambitious efforts is a NASA project called SETI (search for extraterrestrial intelligence). There are various aspects to this search:

● Powerful radio-telescope antennas are deployed to scan radio-frequency bands. These antennas are hooked to advanced computerized receivers that monitor millions of channels simultaneously. At present the antennas are Earth-based but there are plans to park them in orbit and still later on the far side of the moon where there is no interference from Earth-emitted radio activity.

● Using space telescopes astronomers search for planets orbiting distant suns. The goal is to locate planetary systems then scan for signs of life.

● Finally our television transmissions and powerful defense radars continually send out radio waves that travel across Space at the speed of light. It is hoped that if there are advanced civilizations in our part of the galaxy they will pick up these signals.

The search is on. We are sending out signals and we are listening for signs of life.

Will we benefit or suffer from contact with extraterrestrial intelligences?

If in the coming decades a face-to-face contact is made with other intelligences it will be because *they* are advanced enough to reach across interstellar or intergalactic distances. (I doubt that we will have such capabilities before the middle of the twenty-first century.)

It is reasonable to assume that such highly advanced postintelligent beings (non-biological) would have no reason to dominate or harm us. There is nothing we have on this tiny speck in Space that they will not have access to on their own.

A civilization more advanced than ours could help us take cosmic leaps forward. In a matter of weeks or months we could leapfrog a thousand years (twentieth-century Earth-years). Perhaps a million years.

We might be spared all the pain and suffering that we otherwise will inevitably undergo if we evolve on our own.

We might overnight phase out aging and death—the most tragic horror story facing each of us humans.

We might significantly upgrade the level and scope of our intelligence.

We might be helped to convert our absurdly fragile physiologies into more intelligent durable bodies.

We might learn to edit out *all* violence—violence among people and violence among animals.

We might be shown ways to gain quick access to the abundance of the universe.

We might at last learn about the exact origins and size and content and age of our universe or universes.

We might be shown ways to re-create the past—perhaps by reassembling sound and light waves.

We might quickly learn techniques for streaming beyond our solar system to romp around the Milky Way.

Who knows what new skills and information we might acquire as a result of such a connection. Suddenly we will no longer be primitive organisms crawling about on a slab of hostile rock in Space.

We have everything to gain from direct contact with a more advanced stellar civilization.

What about UFOs (unidentified flying objects)?

Does it make sense that superintelligent beings would schlep across millions of light years only to come here and hang around the sky over Orange County?

I can think of no plausible reason why they would show themselves to a few and not to all.

What is Your Ideological Orientation?

1–Do you adhere to a particular ideology: an integrated body of social—economic—political concepts and goals?   ____Yes   ____No

2–What is your social philosophy?
  A–Traditionalist/conservative ("traditional values"): family—faith—work ethic—respect for leadership—patriotism.   ____
  B–Liberal: looser adherence to above values.   ____
  C–Progressive/postindustrial: fluid lifestyles—humanism—leisure ethic—collaborative decision making—globalism.   ____

3–What is your economic ideology?
  A–Capitalism: private or corporate ownership of capital goods. Open-market competition.   ____
  B–Socialism: means of production and distribution of goods controlled by state for common welfare.   ____
  C–Mixed capitalism/socialism.   ____
  D–Postsurvival economics: economics of abundance and immortality.   ____

4–What is your political philosophy?
  A–Dictatorship.   ____
  B–Representative (parliamentary) government.   ____
  C–Direct democracy: voting not for leaders or representatives but directly on issues.   ____

5–What do you foresee as the world's
ideological trend in coming years?

    A–

                              _____Conservative
                              _____Progressive
                              _____Pendulum shifts

    B–

                              _____Right   _____Left
                              _____Beyond right & left

6–Does ideology have any value in our
fluid times?

                              _____Yes   _____No

Answer sheet: MONITOR 20

1   ____Yes (2)   ____No (1)

2 A   ____
   B   ____
   C   ____ (2)

3 A   ____
   B   ____
   C   ____
   D   ____ (2)

4 A   ____
   B   ____
   C   ____ (2)

5 A   ____Conservative   ____Progressive (2) ____Pendulum shifts
   B   ____Right   ____Left   ____Beyond right &
                                                            left (2)

6   ____Yes (2)   ____No

Total: _____

Is there a conservative or liberal trend in the world?

We live in the most revolutionary times in history. Never has human progress been more rapid—global—profound than it is today.

Isn't it often said these days that we live in an age of rapid change? Isn't it the often-heard complaint that things are changing *too fast?*

If things are changing very fast—how then can there be a "conservative trend" anywhere?

The fact is that in our age of lightspeed advances the conservative trend is a myth. There is nothing conservative about our age. There is not even a liberal trend. Conservative and liberal are no longer adequate terms for defining our age of perturbations.

The confluence of rampaging advances on all tracks is revolutionizing everyone and everything. Even conservatives and liberals are continually transformed—often without their own awareness.

Here are some specifics:

1—The conservatives and liberals of today embrace technologies considered futuristic hardly ten years ago.

Until the 1970s embryo transfer—genetic engineering—solar energy—robotics—ultraintelligent machines were still dismissed as science fiction. Today these are thriving industries.

People who only a few years ago approached the "computer" as though it were a tarantula today brag about their home computers.

Until the 1970s "robot" was a stigmatized term imputed to anyone who was seen as cold and estranged. Today robots are glamorous cynosures at conventions and viewed as intelligent and friendly little fellows that do a lot of useful things for us.

How quickly we forget our earlier resistances.

These and other technologies are forward-contexting all areas of life.

2—It is not only new technology that comes on line with increasing rapidity. Conservatives and liberals embrace values and lifestyles considered far-out hardly a decade ago.

"In the past few years there has been much talk of a retreat . . . toward more conservative values—" notes Daniel Yankelovich the respected analyst of social trends in his book *New Rules*. "Our recent studies show evidences of startling cultural changes—changes that penetrate to the very core of American life . . . Tens of millions of women no longer regard having babies as self-fulfilling . . . There are fewer 'typical American families' today than households consisting of a single person—the fastest-growing category of households in the U.S. . . . Vast shifts are taking place in the composition of the workplace . . . For the first time in our history, more women than men were admitted to U.S. institutions of higher learning . . . Change is the only constant."

Even the religious are moving to higher orbits. John Bennett—former president of Union Theological Seminary of New York—recently disclosed a list of seventeen "inhumane" moral stances long espoused by the church leadership that have now been abandoned or are increasingly out of favor. These include: "male superiority—white supremacy— excesses of capitalism—narrow nationalism—support for capital punishment—belief in the inherent sinfulness of sexuality."[1]

American conservatives who until recently supported racial segregation in the southern states today openly condemn apartheid in South Africa.

3—What about political swings to the right in recent U.S. presidential elections?

Things are not as they appear.

• In our age of discontinuity voting conservative may be an attempt to grasp at something familiar and effect a semblance of slowdown.

• In postindustrial societies such as the United States politics is no longer an accurate gauge of a society's moods. In the U.S. nearly half of the eligible voters persistently do not vote. Of those who do vote millions adhere to values and policies that are the antitheses of everything older conservative and liberal politicians stand for. These young generations have vastly different orientations and expectations than the people they vote for. They are like young Catholics who stand in streets and cheer the Pope—then go ahead and defy the church by voting for birth control measures—abortion—the right to divorce—women's rights—high-tech reproductive techniques.

• In countries such as the U.S. where telecommunication is powerful and information spreads laterally government rarely sets the pace. Government is increasingly reactive. The buildup for change coalesces outside politics. (Please see Monitor 8: Power.)

An administration may call itself conservative but the environment in which it operates and which propels it is revolutionary.

4—Finally who are today's conservatives and liberals? They are often business people and investors who unwittingly underwrite the most revolutionary forces in the world.

They are the people who pride themselves on their patriotism yet insist on open-world trade policies and invest in global telecommunication—global transportation—transnational corporations—all of which are helping us outgrow the nation state.

Conservatives and liberals who glorify "the work ethic" invest heav-

ily in "leisure industries" and automated office equipment—
supercomputers—teleconference technology—robots—smart machines
—all of which are helping phase out labor-intensive economies.

Conservatives and old-line liberals who revere family—marriage—
parenthood invest heavily in genetic and reproductive technologies that
this very day are reformatting age-old patterns of procreation and parenthood.

There is nothing conservative about the new economy. This new
high-tech economy transforms everything.

How ironic that the business community which is universally viewed
as conservative is unwittingly among the most revolutionary elements
in the world.

Something new is happening. The world's ideological base is shifting.
In the past when conditions unfolded slowly the world was basically
conservative. As the pace accelerates the world grows more progressive—more future-oriented.

We are all evolving from a basically conservative world to a revolutionary one.

When there is an apparent shift to conservatism in some area—for
example in national elections—it is a "conservative trend" within an
increasingly progressive world.

We are *all* on a fast track.

All humanity is riding a giant escalator. Everyone is continually
moving up. Even those who appear to be standing still and those who
look back.

Traditionalists everywhere are more vocal than ever because the world
is increasingly untraditional.

No government—no political or religious movement—no corporate
interests—no combination of antifuture forces can any longer slow down
the cumulative acceleration of progress.

Whether we call ourselves conservative or liberal—reactionary or
progressive—right or left—we are all swept along by the stampede of
history.

The only trend today is fastforward.

Are we changing too fast?

From the perspective of fifty years *ago* everything is changing very fast in these final years of the century. From the perspective of fifty years *ahead* we are inching forward at a snail's pace.

The fact is that the cumulative speedup of history imposes a tempo of its own. Whether we like it or not the pace of progress will speed up.

Those who are in flow with the thrust of change can contribute significantly to progress. Those who run counter to the flow and attempt to slow things down dissipate their efforts.

As breakthroughs accelerate breakdowns accelerate also. Breakdown of institutions—lifestyles—social and ethical values—technologies— cities—nations. This in turn leads people who see events in slow motion to conclude that the world is falling apart or that we are sliding backward.

How can we cope with runaway breakdowns and breakthroughs?

Most of us instinctively adjust our rate of adaptability. If there were some way we could playback on a screen our personality profiles of twenty years ago we would marvel at how much our adaptibility rates have speeded up to keep pace with advances.

The faster we change the faster our adaptability adapts.

Does ideology have any value in our fluid times?

Ideologies are particularly useful in our times of confusing discontin- uities and accelerations.

An ideology helps bring together ideas and ideals into a unified coherent agenda.

An ideological framework helps clarify concepts—shows the inter- connections among apparently disparate tracks—helps define goals— helps suggest methods for reaching those goals.

In setting forth clear new visions an ideological program can bring hope and act as a rallying force for action.

In our fluid times an ideology can be effective only if it too is fluid—changing and growing and questioning.

What are some highlights of new ideological directions in the coming years?

All existing ideologies of right and left are inherently industrial age. As we hasten to a new age these ideologies lose relevance.

The telespheral age is inevitably spawning new agendas—beyond right and left.

It may be too early to tell exactly how things will fall into place in the coming years. We don't even have a designation for this new ideological thrust.

Years ago I suggested the term "Up-Wing" as the ideological heir to the right- and left-wings. I suggested that Up-Wingers are those who are committed to helping accelerate the shift to new historical and evolutionary levels.

What matters is not so much the name or names we finally settle on for our new agendas. What matters is that we need a new ideological direction.

Right and left ideologies are essentially part of the same industrial-age continuum. In their most progressive leanings they strive to modernize *existing* systems. They call for better family relations—more progressive schools—more sophisticated hospitals—more reliable postal services—more efficient government bureaucracies—more jobs and prosperity—more open elections of government leaders and representatives—cleaner and more efficiently run cities and so on.

Up-Wingers see all these and related systems as inherently outdated. No incremental modernization can effectively salvage these and other industrial-age holdovers. Powerful new forces in the world are steadily rescripting life in fundamentally new ways.

The details of this new age may still be blurred. But the outlines are becoming clearer every day. As noted earlier the direction in *all* areas of life is unmistakably toward decentralization—despecialization—demonopolization—debureaucratization—globalization.

Even more profound evolutionary changes are now evident. We are striving to deanimalize our species—debiologize intelligence—deplanetize.

Following is a short-hand overview of Up-Wing agenda. (For details please see my books *Up-Wingers* and *Telespheres* and the forthcoming *Countdown to Immortality*.)

Physical immortality.

The most urgent problem facing us is not social—economic—political. The most pressing problem facing us *all* everywhere is death.

All other human constraints are derivative.

So long as there is death no one is free. So long as there is death we cannot upgrade the basic quality of life.

The elimination of death has never been on anyone's agenda because throughout the ages we were never able to do anything about it.

Today for the first time ever we are significantly slowing down the aging process. We are devising more and more spare parts for malfunctioning body organs. We are slowly learning to transfer intelligence. Other extraordinary advances are on our launching pads.

Immortality is now a question of when—not if.

The elimination of death will not do away with problems. It will take away the tragedy in human life. Once we attain immortality everything will be possible.

Space colonization.

We must urgently accelerate the tempo of Space exploration and colonization. Why is this a top priority? (I will reiterate for emphasis what I suggested in Monitor 19: Space.)

Space colonization opens up the abundance of the universe.

Frees us of all finiteness.

Quickens the momentum-swing to telespheres.

Accelerates our transformation from Earth-specific animal/human organisms to extraterrestrial posthumans.

Multiplies our chances of connecting with other intelligences who in turn could give us a mighty boost forward.

Telespheres.

Everywhere the industrial world is wearing out. It is not an accident that suddenly more and more of our institutions are malfunctioning. It is not an accident that in advanced industrial societies the nuclear family and school education and postal service and small farms and labor unions and the auto and steel industries and central governments and industrial-age cities and national economies are all buffeted by persistent problems.

These and other industrial-age systems are all interconnected. As one part of the apparatus breaks down other parts begin to fall apart also.

The fact is that the entire planet is shifting to a new stage—beyond industrialism. But the right and left—the two dominant ideological thrusts of our times—do not have agendas to facilitate a quick and coordinated stepup to the postindustrial age.

The differences between the industrial and the telespheral worlds are basic and significant. By grafting intelligence and telecommunication to all areas of our lives we are forever altering the nature of everything: our services—our employment—our ways of interacting with one another—our decision-making processes.

Telespheres forge a continuous interface of people and technology and services. In this emerging electronic environment we do not need the cumbersome bureaucracies and structures of the industrial age. We have *direct* access to services—at any time and from anywhere.

The most "progressive" school is still an old system of education. The stage beyond school education is teleducation.

The most modern hospital is still an old and inefficient way of keeping people healthy. The stage beyond hospitals is preventive protective telemedicine.

The most efficient postal service is still postal. The stage beyond is electronic mail.

In other words the most modern automobile is still an automobile. A truly modern transport is something beyond the automobile—a helicopter or a magnetic levitation device.

We need to leap to the next stage.

Networks of intimacy.
Mating—reproduction—parenting are undergoing profound changes.

The conditions that through the ages sustained family systems are on their way out. People no longer need to marry for procreation —companionship — love — sexual intimacy — protection — economic support.

We are steadily moving toward shared or collaborative procreation and collaborative parenting.

Collaborative procreation means screening people's sex cells and using only those most likely to produce healthy wholesome new lives. This will upgrade the quality of life for everybody.

Shared parenting means creating collaborative networks of people who wish to share in the parenting of children. At a time when many marriages break up and people value their autonomy such networks free people of the responsibility of parenting alone. These arrangements allow parents freedom of movement. They also allow children a richer more varied more continuous early environment.

Postsurvival economics.

Until now all economic systems have dealt with survival. How to provide for people's basic needs: food—shelter—clothing.

The basics of all economics have not changed in hundreds of thousands of years. The economics of Neanderthals and the economics of a modern complex society are essentially the same. The details have grown more complex—but the basics are unchanged. How to provide for people's basic needs—survival needs.

Something unprecedented is happening in economics.

We are going beyond mere survival.

The new economics—the economics of the coming decades—deals not with survival. The new economics wants to insure our immortality.

Some of the fastest-growing areas in economics today (and certainly in the years ahead) are technologies and resources that directly or indirectly aim at the indefinite extension of each human life.

What are some of these glamor areas of modern economics? Molecular biology—bioengineering—biochips—prostheses—body reconstruction—geriatrics and gerontology—life-extending products—medical technology—life support technology—life suspension.

Other areas of postsurvival economics: supercomputers—robots—androids—replicants—ultraintelligent systems—memory transfer and so on.

Some of these technologies are already multibillion-dollar industries. The others are on their way.

The new economics does not strive to keep people alive for a few decades. It aims to extend each life indefinitely.

Up-Wing economics is not content with cradle-to-grave protection. It wants to do away with the grave.

The new economics goes beyond mere survival.

What we have here is the beginnings of a twenty-first-century Economics of Immortality.

Collaborative decision-making (politics).

Voting for leaders in free elections has long been touted as a "democratic process."

The fact is that this is an anachronistic definition of democracy. Voting for leaders—even in free elections—is not democracy. A system of government that calls for a few officials to make unilateral decisions for millions of people can hardly be called democratic.

Government through leadership and representation—right or left—elected or imposed—is a form of private enterprise with its own vested interests—its own self-serving ideological and economic advantages—its unilateral exercise of power—the inevitable cult of personality.

Government through leadership automatically creates two distinct categories—leaders and followers. This in turn leads to unequal exercise of power.

Whether the right or the left wins elections does not redress this undemocratic imbalance. The decisions are still made by the leaders. (Governments in advanced industrial countries are losing power—not because of right or left reforms—but because of the decentralizing impact of the new information flow.)

The only way to transfer power to the people is to phase out all systems of government based on leadership and representation. Democracy in our times means voting—not for leaders—but voting directly on issues.

This may not have been possible in the past. But today we have the electronic technology for such collaborative decision-making.

The growing number of referendums—ballot initiatives—propositions—public opinion polls are steps toward the eventual creation of a political framework enabling people to participate *directly* in decision making.

Collaborative self-government is not only more democratic than all existing political systems. It is also a more rapid—efficient—depoliticized way of making decisions in our times.

These are some Up-Wing goals and priorities. There are others: globalism—telecommunities—twenty-first-century values and so on.

All the above priorities are interconnected. To advance rapidly in any one area we must leap ahead in *all* areas.

This new ideological trajectory is intended to bring us more freedom more abundance more leisure more fluidity more intimacy more growth.

Today as we hasten toward telespherization and global life—toward new sources of limitless abundance and new forms of limitless intelligence—toward transsolar colonies and immortality—we are reaching beyond conservative and liberal—beyond right and left.

We are moving Up.

How Future Oriented Are You?

1–Do you think about the future? The next five years? The next twenty?

____Often   ____Sometimes
____Never

2–Do you think of the Big Picture? Who are we? What is all this about? Where are we going?

____Often   ____Sometimes
____Never

3–Do you actually design long-range plans (two to twenty years) for yourself and/or for your organization?

____Often   ____Sometimes
____Never

4–Do you think that it is useless to plan ahead because we cannot make accurate forecasts?

____Yes   ____No

5–Do you think we should "live in the present"—the future will take care of itself?

____Yes   ____No

6–Where do you stand in relation to progressive changes? Are you generally behind the times? In flow with the pace of change? Generally ahead?

____Behind   ____In flow
____Ahead

7–How much emphasis do you place on people's past? Where were you born? Who were your parents? Where did you grow up? Where did you study? Where have you worked?

____Much emphasis
____Mild emphasis
____No interest

8–Are there any "eternal values"— values that never change?

____Yes   ____No

9–Do you have a religious (or spiritual) orientation?

____Yes   ____No

A–Do you believe in fate or destiny?	___Yes	___No
B–Is it all in the hands of a god?	___Yes	___No
C–Is it all predicted in the Bible or Old Testament or Koran?	___Yes	___No
D–Are religions declining or spreading?	___Declining	___Spreading

10–Are you a secular humanist—an atheist—an evolutionist?	___Yes	___No
A–For example: Do you believe that we are free agents in the universe and that our future is in our own hands?	___Yes	___No

11–Are you actively involved with any future-oriented organizations? For example:

A–Alternative lifestyles: singles networks—mobilia—group parenting—etc.?	___Yes	___No
B–Abundance projects: solar energy—nuclear fusion—hydroponics—etc.?	___Yes	___No
C–Globalist organizations: Planetary Citizens—global travel (groups)—global language—etc.?	___Yes	___No
D–Ultraintelligent systems: robots —androids—supercomputers—etc.?	___Yes	___No
E–Life extension organizations: Anti-aging—cryonic suspension—immortality—etc.?	___Yes	___No
F–Space-related organizations: Space program—Space colonies —exobiology?	___Yes	___No
G–Normative movements: Up-Wingers—Futurist groups—etc.?	___Yes	___No

Answer sheet: MONITOR 21

1   ____Often (2)   ____Sometimes   ____Never

2   ____Often (2)   ____Sometimes (1)   ____Never

3   ____Often (2)   ____Sometimes (1)   ____Never

4   ____Yes   ____No (2)

5   ____Yes   ____No (2)

6   ____Behind   ____In flow (1)   ____Ahead (2)

7   ____Much emphasis   ____Mild emphasis (2)   ____No interest (1)

8   ____Yes   ____No (2)

9   ____Yes   ____No (2)
   A   ____Yes   ____No (2)
   B   ____Yes   ____No (2)
   C   ____Yes   ____No (2)
   D   ____Declining (2)   ____Spreading

10   ____Yes (2)   ____No
   A   ____Yes (2)   ____No

11 A   ____Yes (2)   ____No
   B   ____Yes (2)   ____No
   C   ____Yes (2)   ____No
   D   ____Yes (2)   ____No
   E   ____Yes (2)   ____No
   F   ____Yes (2)   ____No
   G   ____Yes (2)   ____No

Total: _____

Shouldn't we "live in the present"?

What is the present? Today? Today will be the past in a few hours.

This week? This week will be over in a couple of days.

You cannot live in the present. You can only live for the future. All life is movement toward the future.

People who claim to live in the present actually live in the past.

For planners in particular there is no present. You cannot plan for the present. The present has no pragmatic value.

The concept of a "present" is a carryover from past centuries. In slow-track times the idea of "the present" may have had some meaning. The present was an identifiable time frame for historians and sociologists and planners. The present may have stretched for forty or fifty years —an average lifetime.

In our runaway times the present is no longer a useful time frame. Last month's information has already oxidized. By next year the rampage of new information and advances will have produced a new context. In two years most current textbooks will have atrophied.

The present is a myth. (Force of habit may cause us to use the term. Just as we still say "sunset" though we know that the sun does not set.)

There is only a past and a future.

There is not much we can do about the past. We can do much about the future. We can help create it.

How much emphasis do you place on the past?

In the past societies were past-oriented. Emphasis was on traditions and ancient holy books and people's origins. Whose son are you? What village do you come from? How many verses can you recite from such and such old book? Where were you baptized?

The orientation is shifting. Societies are increasingly future oriented. Partly because obsolescence sets in quickly there is less and less emphasis on the past.

Where you grew up—who your parents were—what degrees you acquired twenty years ago—reveal less and less about who you are today. It is not how downdated you are but how updated.

Not surprisingly the emphasis in *modern* psychotherapy is less on a person's past and more on today and tomorrow.

You can tell a lot about the orientation of a society or people by the questions they ask.

Planning ahead.

We are just emerging from ages during which we rarely planned ahead. We did not understand the dynamics of change. Our concepts of cause and effect were absurdly faulty. And we were too locked into the daily struggle for survival to have the luxury of planning ahead.

At most we planned for the next harvest. The prevailing attitude was: "Whatever god wants" or "Whatever fate has in store."

This passivity—though phasing out—is still with us. For many people today planning for the future means "Who am I having dinner with this Friday night?"

It is precisely because we do not plan ahead that we rush headlong into a high-voltage romance only to discover with much pain that the person in whose orbit we are caught is on an incompatible trajectory.

It is precisely because students do not plan ahead intelligently that they discover three years later that they had been marinating in the wrong academic concoction.

It is precisely because corporations do not plan ahead intelligently that they suddenly discover that they have frittered away millions on a product that no longer has a market—or that is undersold by similar products from cross-global competitors.

It is precisely because cities do not plan ahead intelligently that entire neighborhoods suddenly decompose into slums or that the urban sprawl is hobbled overnight by a geriatric transportation system.

It is precisely because nations do not plan ahead intelligently that people are undernourished or cannot find adequate housing or face costly medical expenses.

Planning for the future is a sure sign of intelligence.

Predicting the future with increasing accuracy.

Something startling is happening in human affairs. We are predicting the future with increasing accuracy.

A capability that we had long attributed to gods—prophets—clairvoyants is now enjoyed by forecasters using the magic wand of science and technology.

This new skill is steadily revolutionizing the way we approach our problems and our potentials. In time this new tool will profoundly transform all areas of our lives.

How do we go about forecasting?

First: Each discipline (weather forecasting—economics—demographics—etc.) is developing specific methodologies to deal with the dynamics of change in that field.

Second: We are relying on new technology to help us gather information—test it—process it—cross-factor it. We deploy monitors—remote sensing—data banks—modeling and simulation—expert systems—global information networks—so on.

It is precisely because the weather service deploys an array of fancy high-tech that weather forecasts are now about ninety percent accurate.

Other technologies are helping us fine-tune forecasts in politics—genetics—psychology—urban studies—economics—earthquake activity—cosmology.

This growing ability to scan ahead is helping us plan intelligently for the future.

Are there any eternal (constant) values?

There are no constant or eternal values. The idea of constancy comes from an antiquated view of a stable or static world.

Values change as the environment changes. Values cannot be decoupled from other forces in society: economics—social life—technology.

Values change roughly at the same rate as technological change.

Resistances to new technology are just as tenacious and widespread as resistances to new values. In fact people resist new technology mainly because a change of hardware inevitably brings a change of pace and lifestyle and values.

Yet people everywhere assume that new technology and changing world conditions unfold against a backdrop of never-changing values. As though values existed in a vacuum.

For example conservative leaders in the United States and in Europe push for new technology and resources yet stress the need to hold on to "traditional values."

Saudi Arabian leaders import billions of dollars of new technology yet insist that they do not want their "sacred traditions" tampered with.

Parents in slow communities around the planet send their offspring to faraway universities to study social sciences and world affairs and nuclear physics yet caution them not to forget their "traditional way of life."

Does any of this make sense? Is it possible to have communication satellites—global television—supercomputers—supersonic transports —birth control devices and still hold on to "traditional values"?

The new technology and the global economy are playing havoc with traditions everywhere in the world.

Love—loyalty—respect—success—unity—responsibility—sacrifice—efficiency—truth—integrity—all these meant one thing at one time. They mean something else today. They will mean something radically different in twenty or thirty years.

For example at one time holding on to a career—a job—a home for a lifetime was considered a sign of responsibility. The person who changed spouses—jobs—careers was considered irresponsible and unstable.

In our times such continuity is not only increasingly difficult. It is not even desirable. We now value the person who is able to retool and move on.

Our perceptions of success and failure are also changing.

For hundreds of years *any* rich or famous or powerful person was considered successful. Success for men meant making a lot of money or reaching the top of the bureaucratic ladder. Nobody bothered to question the quality of such people's lives.

Success for women meant "landing a husband." Rarely was the quality of the marriage questioned.

Our concepts of success have changed as evidenced by the number of people who have dropped out of the bureaucratic rat race and the tens of millions of women and men who are not marrying—or who disconnect if the quality of the marriage is not to their liking.

We now gauge success by new standards: How much self-fulfillment is there in your life? How much personal growth? Creativity? Leisure?

What about loyalty—purity—faithfulness in "relationships"? At one time this meant not ever making love with anyone except your spouse. In our fluid times sexual loyalty often means confining yourself to one lover for a few weeks or months or a couple of years. For millions of men and women who have multiple lovers sexual loyalty has no meaning at all. (The current sexual retrenchment brought on by the fear of AIDS is temporary. Before long a cure will be found for AIDS. But the shifts in values are long-term and in my view irreversible.)

We are tampering with even more fundamental truths—''absolute truths.''

For example until recent times death was final and irreversible. Once a person died—that was it. This was an ''absolute truth''—a ''universal truth.'' In our times thousands of people are brought back from death —through cardiopulmonary resuscitation and other techniques. What was an absolute truth is no longer so absolute.

At one time ''leaving this world'' meant dying. To the religious it meant going to a heaven or a hell. If you were not in this world you were dead. This too was an absolute truth. In our times people routinely liftoff in spacecraft and freefall *outside this world*. Months later they reenter our world.

More and more such ''eternal verities'' will be reversed in the coming years. As these basic ''constants'' change our social values and ethics change also.

The fact that our ''eternal'' truths and social values change is reason for hope. It proves the dynamism of us humans.

Is there a resurgence of religion in the world?

Religion is in a more rapid decline today than at any time in history. Until a few decades ago religions dominated all areas of life in all societies. Nearly everyone in North America and Europe was a churchgoer. Nearly everyone in the Moslem world was a fundamentalist. Nearly every Jew—by today's standards—was orthodox.

Even a quick scan of early twentieth-century newspapers and journals will show a pervasive climate of religion and the power of the clergy.

The decline of the traditional family—the rapid rise in divorce—the loosening up of sexual mores—open homosexuality—legalized abortion—widespread use of birth control measures—the rapid spread of the women's movement—the phaseout of patriarchy—these are a few evidences of the declining influence of religion.

Tens of millions of Catholics around the world now openly flout the Vatican's rulings on abortion and birth control and women's rights. This would have been unheard-of just a few decades ago.

Tens of millions of young educated Moslems scattered in the big cities of the world have never been inside a mosque and have never observed Koranic tenets on daily prayers—marriage laws—non-drinking—fasting—pilgrimage. They are Moslem only in name.

Year after year scores of churches and synagogues in the United States and Europe give way to apartment buildings—cinemas—shopping malls. They are never replaced.

Recently Hans Kung the Roman Catholic theologian addressing the American Psychiatric Association conference in Washington, D.C. complained that "the large majority" of psychiatrists simply ignore religion in treating patients. In fact some go so far as to view their patients' expressions of religion as "an illness requiring a cure."[1]

The internationally known theologian went on to say that "in Freud's time religion was fought over and argued about, but today there is silence on religion from psychiatry—religion is the final taboo."

There is "silence on religion" precisely because religion has ceased to be a factor in more and more people's lives.

One way to obtain a quick readout on the way the world is going is to observe the youth. It does not take advanced radars to see that the youth of the world is rapidly moving away from religion.

Why the decline of religion?

1—Religions are inherently authoritarian. They demand unquestioning adherence to absolute commandments that are said to have been set down by gods or prophets. Such a system built on faith and total acceptance worked well during humanity's childhood—the thousands of years during which people everywhere grew up in authoritarian/ paternalistic environments that demanded submissiveness.

In our times entire generations are growing up in environments inclined to reciprocity. They are conditioned to question and challenge and take part in decision making. The paternalism and absolutism of religions are alien to their emotional reference.

It is startling to hear people talk of "freedom of religion." Religion itself is unfree. What some people want is the right to be unfree.

2—Religions thrived for thousands of years mainly because they brought comfort and hope at a time when life was largely a relentless cycle of suffering. They offered support and love to those who felt unloved or abandoned. They offered reassuring rationales for people's misfortunes. Religions gave them goals and direction and purpose in life. Most religions even promised some kind of everlasting life after death.

There is still much suffering in the world. But in the more advanced areas of our planet the level of suffering is steadily receding. Hunger —privation—crippling diseases—onslaughts of nature—high death rate—these are not common realities of modern life. Most people can cope on their own with their problems.

For those who cannot cope the modern world offers numerous therapeutic supports such as networks of friendships—professional and creative fulfillments—psychotherapy—hypnotherapy—counseling . . . These comforting therapies work better in the modern world than the simplistic palliatives of religion.

3—Religions—like other absolutist systems that demand total acceptance—depend on information monopoly for their survival. Authoritarian movements always insist on determining what information should be made available to people.

But we live in what has been called the "information age." Information is all around us. It gushes out from countless sources. It is increasingly difficult to control information—manipulate it—shut it down. In such an information-intensive environment religion has more and more difficulty exercising unilateral influence.

Every day the sciences are expanding our knowledge base. Each time we learn a little more about the origins of our universe and the solar system and our planet we undermine the basic premises and causalities of religion. Each time we learn a little more about the genesis of living organisms in the oceans and the origins of primates and hominids and the evolution of intelligence and speech we undermine the basic premises and dogmas of religions.

The cumulative buildup of this secular information-environment has its greatest impact on youth.

If religions are declining what accounts for the rise of fundamentalism in some parts of the world?

There is no resurgence of religion anywhere in the world. If it appears as if there is a rise in fundamentalism it is because of the following factors:

1—Sunday evangelists—Jewish fundamentalists—ayatollahs have long been around. Global television has made them more visible—giving the impression that they are proliferating. (The high visibility of tele-vangelists on national television will not—as is often assumed—help spread religion. The more religion comes out into the open the more quickly it will decline.)

2—The global comingling of people is spreading. In recent years millions of people from less advanced (and therefore more religious) societies have moved to North America and Europe briefly swelling the ranks of worshipers.

3—As religions steadily lose relevance and secular ideas spread across the planet the religious feel more threatened and therefore grow more vocal. Whenever an established order faces decline its guardians fight back ferociously giving the impression of a sudden resurgence. For example British feelings for their empire were probably never more impassioned than in the late 1940s and the 1950s when the empire was collapsing everywhere.

Future-oriented and normative movements.

These movements as a rule are not focused on problems or issues of the past. For example they are not *directly* involved with such age-old problems as poverty—hunger—violence—wars.

Most of these movements are geared to the future. They start off with new premises—ask new questions—aim for new answers—point to new goals.

They are seminal and visionary.

In striving for new norms the people in these movements fully expect that age-old problems will automatically be subsumed.

For example in pushing to develop new sources of limitless energy such as solar and fusion and hydrogen they believe that the inexpensive and abundant energy will do away with age-old poverty—imbalances in wealth—recessions—inflations.

But these future-oriented activists have their sights on more ambitious goals.

They believe that the new post-fossil-fuel abundance reinforced by the new global economy—the new Space environment—the new post-scarcity values will inevitably lead to a new economic order free of the constraints of money and labor-for-wages and the psychology of ownership.

Long-range planners talk of twenty-first-century replicators—Santa Claus machines—infinity systems.

Other future-oriented activists have similarly lofty goals. The creation of postfamily lifestyles—the colonization of the solar system—immortality and so on. These long-range efforts will not only defuse age-old problems and limitations. They will actually advance us to a fundamentally higher order of life.

How Optimistic Or Pessimistic Are You About The Future?

1–Are you pessimistic about the future of humanity?   ___Yes   ___No

    A–Do you believe that conditions in the world have been deteriorating in recent times?   ___Yes   ___No

    B–Are we heading toward a major global cataclysm?   ___Yes   ___No

    C–Do you dread the future?   ___Yes   ___No

    D–Do you wonder if there will even be a future?   ___Yes   ___No

2–Are you optimistic about the future?   ___Yes   ___No

    A–Do you believe that things have been improving for humanity in recent times?   ___Yes   ___No

    B–Will we continue to make progress?   ___Yes   ___No

    C–Do you expect major breakthroughs in the coming years that will significantly improve human life?   ___Yes   ___No

    D–Do you look forward to the future?   ___Yes   ___No

3–Do you believe that conditions swing back and forth—like a pendulum—sometimes we progress other times we regress?   ___Yes   ___No

4–Does it finally matter whether one is an optimist or a pessimist?   ___Yes   ___No

5–Are you neither an optimist nor a pessimist but a realist?   ___Realist
    ___Realist pessimist
    ___Realist optimist

Answer sheet: MONITOR 22

1		____Yes	____No (2)
	A	____Yes	____No (2)
	B	____Yes	____No (2)
	C	____Yes	____No (2)
	D	____Yes	____No (2)

2		____Yes (2)	____No
	A	____Yes (2)	____No
	B	____Yes (2)	____No
	C	____Yes (2)	____No
	D	____Yes (2)	____No

3   ____Yes   ____No (2)

4   ____Yes (2)   ____No

5 ____Realist   ____Realist   ____Realist optimist
                          pessimist   (2)

Total: _____

Are you neither an optimist nor a pessimist—but a realist?

If you think that you are neither an optimist nor a pessimist but a realist you are—full of jet exhaust.

I have never met a self-styled realist who did not have a pessimistic or optimistic bias.

The optimist and the pessimist each believes that it is the realist. Each offers a litany of reasons to justify its outlook.

For example the pessimist maintains that "the U.S. and the Soviet Union are building up their arsenals. Neither side will give in. There are many paranoid people on both sides. Sooner or later frictions are bound to get out of hand. We will inevitably blow ourselves up. I am not a pessimist or anything—just a realist.''

The optimist is just as adamant. ''There has not been a major war since World War II several decades ago. Remote monitoring makes sneak attacks increasingly difficult. Every day the infrastructures the economics the technology and the psychology of global cohesion are spreading. The world today is more interconnected than ever. Even during a freeze in U.S./Soviet relations there are more joint projects going on than at any time in the past. I see us moving toward cooperation—not war. This is not optimism—it is sound realism.''

We are back where we were—optimism versus pessimism.

Obviously neither optimism nor pessimism can be categorical. We just don't know. Things could go either way in *every* area of life.

Does it really matter whether one is an optimist or a pessimist?

Some people are energized by hope and good news. Others feel challenged by bad news.

An environment that is relentlessly pessimistic undermines the self-confidence of people—particularly of children. Persistent pessimism about the world and the future can lead to withdrawal and apathy.

''What is the use of trying? Human nature is hopelessly evil—the world is rotten—the future is bleak. Why try? The hell with the world.''

It is difficult to motivate people who have grown up in a climate of despair—people for whom things never worked out or who were made to feel that things can never work out.

People who grow up in supportive can-do environments are more likely to have confidence in themselves and in the world and therefore be more inclined to appreciate humanity's advances and deal energetically with problems.

As a rule optimists are more likely to be future oriented than pessimists.

Are people generally optimistic or pessimistic?

There are more pessimists than optimists. We complain more than we rejoice. We brood more than we exult.

Bad news is more serious than good news. Therefore we take the pessimists and the alarmists among us more seriously than our few optimists. Doomsayers have always had a greater following than have the optimists.

It is easier to be a pessimist than an optimist. The reasons are obvious:

—We are surrounded by problems.

—We have all grown up in neurotic anxiety-ridden environments that instilled in us guilt and shame and self-doubt.

—Each of us is a fragile organism that can at any moment die— forever.

I do not know of an optimistic people in the world.

Aren't Americans said to be an optimistic people?

Modern Americans are certainly less fatalistic and self-doubting than people on other continents. In fact as economic hardships and social restrictions lessen in the world people everywhere grow more confident and hopeful.

But Americans are far from optimistic. Most Americans in fact tend to be crisis oriented. They act like doomsday junkies who seem to need a daily dose of bad news to keep going.

The American news media with the help of everyone churns out one crisis after another and the people as though suffering from a national Alzheimer's memory-lapse respond to each and every self-manipulation.

Switch back to the 1950s for a moment. America was in the grips of a Communist hysteria. The kind of hysteria you would expect to find among voodoo aborigines who had just been told that a people-eating ogre had been set loose among them.

While the world watched in disbelief America put on a bizarre ritual-dance of panic. A repressive atmosphere swept across this country. People who did not have the foggiest idea what "Communism" stood for whispered the word as though they were referring to the plague. Those suspected of collusion with the "evil godless Commies" were hounded out of their jobs their homes their communities. Tens of thousands of Americans were stampeded into building bomb shelters as protection from the *imminent* Communist invasion.

At first everyone's favorite enemy was the Soviet Union. Then Red China was given the honor of public enemy number one. Every evil intent was imputed to the "hordes" of Communist China. "The U.S.

is a superpower that becomes panic-stricken at the mere rustle of leaves in the world—'' said Mao Tse-tung.

By the late 1960s much of the world had established diplomatic or trade relations with China and the U.S. had no option but to go along and recognize the existence of the world's most populous state.

Overnight the hate campaign evaporated. The very people who had spoken of the "wicked godless yellow menace" now fell all over themselves rushing to China as tourists as campaigning politicians and as business executives panting to close multibillion-dollar deals.

Such overreaction is by no means confined to politics and the international scene. The U.S. seems to go from one "crisis" to another: the ecology scare—the pollution hysteria—the ozone-depletion alarm —the SST furor—the Population Bomb.

The Population Bomb? All through the 1960s and the 1970s neo-Malthusians insisted that the world population was proliferating so rapidly that "soon there will be no room for anyone to lie down." A Stanford University professor made headlines and best-seller lists with such apocalyptic predictions as: "The battle to feed all of humanity is over . . . In the 1970s hundreds of millions of people are going to starve to death . . . At this late date nothing can prevent a substantial increase in the world death rate . . ." Meanwhile every global report showed that the world "population explosion" was slowing down.

In the early 1970s there was the "oil crisis." Americans were told that they were descending into a new "Dark Age." Politicians— newscasters—academicians—Nobel Prize winners and other "authorities" announced that the world would soon run out of oil—that we had "finite resources" and that we had reached the "limits to growth." Over and over Americans were told by the specialists that they would have to make *permanent*—repeat *permanent*—adjustments in their lifestyles because they would "never enjoy the old levels of prosperity."

"We are probably entering an age of scarcity," Howard K. Smith of *ABC Evening News* announced in February 1974. "But I don't believe that is bad. It is an axiom that disciplined children are happier than nondisciplined ones. The same is true of nations." Did he mean that scarcity is good for us?

The immolations over the "energy crisis" had hardly ceased when Americans were served up a new crisis—the genetic engineering show. Every day newspapers and magazines and television programs carried cataclysmic predictions by opinion-makers—Nobel Prize winners and other "authorities" that the new recombinant DNA technology would produce new forms of bacterial life that would escape from the laboratory and "destroy millions of human lives."

This "crisis" was followed by the herpes scare. Americans were told that herpes was more insidious than other sexually transmitted diseases. "Herpes is an epidemic of major proportions and will continue to spread"—that was an oft-repeated news bulletin. Evangelists of doom and other moralists had a field day. "This is God's way of punishing you for your wicked promiscuous ways." For a while many people stopped making love and swimming in public pools.

Next Americans enjoyed the Nuclear War hysteria. Feature films— TV series—radio interviews—instant books—daily newspaper headlines were all suddenly riveted on only one topic: Imminent Global Nuclear War. While the rest of the world went about its business America was caught up in another ritual frenzy. It was widely reported that children all over the USA had recurrent nightmares about the bomb and the end of the world.

Then there was the terrorism panic. While the streets and outdoor cafes of Europe and North Africa overflowed with revelers millions of Americans canceled their travel plans.

Then the Missing Children Panic—the hysteria over drugs—the panic over chemicals—on and on and on . . .

What will Americans be gloomy about next week? What will people beat themselves with? What new crisis? What is the new Saturday Night Horror Show?

Has anybody ever done a study to find out how long Americans could survive without a major "crisis"? Eight minutes? Twenty-six minutes? Would everyone start to panic if no new crisis could be staged? Would the entire country be put on an emergency no-crisis alert?

The overreaction to these "crises" are part of the same psychology as the anti-Communist hysteria. In each case the pattern is the same: Overstate the problem—blow it out of proportion to what it really is —play on people's fears and anxieties. Milk each issue for what it's worth—then move on to another "crisis."

This tendency to fabricate and exaggerate is not confined to any one group in the ideological spectrum. Conservatives are paranoid about Communism. Liberals exaggerate the war issue. Many environmentalists overstate problems of the ecology. Sunday evangelists put out "end-of-the-world'' five-alarms on almost everything. ''Primal screamers'' are everywhere.

I do not suggest that we are without problems. There are plenty of problems. Industrial pollution is a problem. Alcoholism and drug addiction are problems. The nuclear arms race is a problem. AIDS and herpes are problems. America's anachronistic gunboat diplomacy—the heavy-handed intervention in other countries—that too is a problem.

It is the tendency to exaggerate and overplay problems that I find manipulative and in the long run counterproductive. It is the people's gullibility—or is it receptivity?—that is also baffling.

How can millions of people allow themselves to be manipulated time and time and again by such obviously transparent scare tactics? You would think that by now everyone in America would have wised up and refused to go along.

Could it be that people here thrive on such panic-mongering?

Why are Americans—perhaps more than other people—so obsessed with crises?

—Is ''crisis'' big business? In a country where everything is for profit is crisis profitable? There is no question that a lot of people in this country make a lot of money manufacturing and peddling crises: newspapers are said to sell more briskly when disasters or scandals are hyped up. Films and television reap profits from disaster stories—real and fictional. Religions thrive on people's anxieties and fears. The entire security industry makes billions in firearms and locks—guard rails and electronic alarm systems. Militarism is probably the biggest business of all. Over 30,000 private companies in the U.S. thrive on military expenditures. ''Preparing for war'' is good business.

—Is this receptivity to crisis-mongering an outgrowth of the old puritanism—guilt and self-hate? At one time Sunday evangelists all over America told the people how wicked they were and scared the hell out of them with graphic descriptions of the imminent end of the world. Today others do essentially the same thing—make people feel bad about themselves and punish them with horror stories. In other words do people here need a daily fix of bad news to keep them going? Is this what people feel they *deserve?* Is there a pathological need for enemies?

What are some of the consequences of this perpetual atmosphere of crisis?

• As noted earlier a chronically negative environment often leads to loss of confidence in one's self—in society and in the future. This can be particularly damaging to children who tend to take things at face value and do not have the perspective to see that everything is exaggerated.

• Such a venomous atmosphere causes people to distrust everyone. Individuals and nations with leftist ideologies are considered "evil." Other people are to be avoided because they may carry sexual diseases. Yet others may molest or steal your children. Of course caution is necessary at times but exaggerated distrust may itself create problems.

• Another fallout is the loss of trust in the news media and in public officials. No wonder many people in this country refuse to read newspapers or watch newscasts. "There is nothing but bad news."

• When everything is hyped up it is difficult to maintain perspective and deal intelligently with problems. Because problems are often exaggerated the responses are inevitably exaggerated. For example the overkill to the arms race generates nightmares and depression in people—and this becomes a problem in itself. The overreaction to problems of the environment in the early 1970s caused the U.S. to abandon the development of a supersonic passenger aircraft.

• Finally in the U.S. the people's outlook on the future—the mood of the country—is perpetually tainted by the crisis of the day.

"How are you?"

"I am very worried about this terrible problem of the ozone."

Switch forward a few weeks: "With all this terrorism going around—I am really scared to go anywhere."

A few weeks later: "How can one feel safe when they are tampering with people's genetic makeup?"

A couple of months later: "How can I feel good about anything? We are going to blow ourselves up."

We have problems—real problems. We do not need to fabricate crises or exaggerate the severity of existing problems.

Overkill is not an effective way of dealing with anything.

Does the quickening pace of progress justify optimism about our future?

In my view social—economic—political progress does not by itself justify optimism about our human situation or our future. The *basic* human condition remains largely unchanged. We still experience pain and suffering—and we die.

In my books *Optimism One* (1969) and *Up-Wingers* (1972) I wrote: "So long as we are hopelessly doomed to finite life spans and trapped within a small speck in Space all our social economic political freedoms are limited and ultimately meaningless."

I went on to suggest that something new is unfolding in the human condition—something unprecedented—something beyond historical progress—something potentially full of hope.

"Suddenly the barriers are coming down. Suddenly humankind's situation is not circumscribed or limited . . . We are no longer confined to this tiny planet. Soon we will no longer be confined to our fragile mortal bodies. We are on our way to becoming universal and immortal.

"This is precisely the distinction between the new optimism and the optimism of the visionaries of the past. The optimism of a Goethe a Nietzsche or a Marx was necessarily a limited optimism based on historical progress. It was an optimism within a basically pessimistic human situation.

"But the optimism I have been advancing (since the early 1960s) is not based simply on historical progress. It is primarily and ultimately predicated on our evolutionary breakthroughs.

"To miss this central point is to miss the meaning of this late twentieth-century optimism.

"In our preoccupation with daily domestic problems we tend to lose sight of these transcendent dimensions now opening up to us. It is therefore not surprising that we persist in our traditional pessimism.

"But the philosophy of an age cannot and must not be derived from daily newspaper headlines . . . An age cannot be defined by the detail of everyday events. The broader currents are what finally mark an age.

"These broad and ever-broadening currents mark ours as the First Age of Optimism."

What Is Your Level Of Humanity?

1–Do you approve of corporal punishment? ____Yes ____No

2–Should people have the right to own firearms? ____Yes ____No

3–Are you in favor of the death penalty—for *any* crime? ____Yes ____No

4–Do you hunt or fish? ____Yes ____No

5–Do you eat meat—including poultry and fish? ____Yes ____No

6–Do you wear furs or approve of people's wearing furs? ____Yes ____No

7–Do you participate in—or enjoy watching—violent "sports": boxing —American football—rugby— wrestling—martial arts—bullfighting? ____Yes ____No

8–Do you watch films and TV shows that emphasize or glorify violence? ____Yes ____No

9–Do you lend support to Amnesty International in its efforts to stop torture and execution of prisoners around the world? ____Yes ____No

10–Do you contribute to relief efforts for victims of famines—earthquakes—floods and other disasters? ____Yes ____No

11–Do you approve of military invasion or bombing of a nation by another —for *any* reason? ____Yes   ____No

12–Do you support any expression of violence (terrorism—kidnapping— assassination—etc.) for a *just* cause? ____Yes   ____No

13–Are you in favor of a continued arms buildup to keep up in the arms race? ____Yes   ____No

14–Are you *particularly* outraged when violence is directed at your nation— race—ethnic group? ____Yes   ____No

    A–Are you *equally* outraged at violence directed at *any* people anywhere in the world? ____Yes   ____No

Answer sheet: MONITOR 23

1   ____Yes   ____No (2)

2   ____Yes   ____No (2)

3   ____Yes   ____No (2)

4   ____Yes   ____No (2)

5   ____Yes   ____No (2)

6   ____Yes   ____No (2)

7   ____Yes   ____No (2)

8   ____Yes   ____No (2)

9   ____Yes (2)   ____No

10   ____Yes (2)   ____No

11   ____Yes   ____No (2)

12   ____Yes   ____No (2)

13   ____Yes   ____No (2)

14   ____Yes   ____No (2)
   A   ____Yes (2)   ____No

Total: _____

Our level of humanity.

You can gauge your level of humanity by asking yourself questions such as those on the question sheet.

You can tell a lot about a person's level of humanity by that person's attitude toward violence and punishment and respect for life.

"Beware of those in whom the need to punish is strong"—wrote Goethe.

Are you punitive or reformist? Vindictive or forgiving?

How compassionate are you toward *all* living creatures?

How sensitive are you to the fragility of *all* life?

Do you empathize only with members of your family—ethnic group—nation? Or do you empathize with people everywhere?

You may be a friendly person and call yourself humane or spiritual —but if you support the death penalty or support violence for *any* cause or identify only with members of your own national or ethnic group and disregard the humanity of others or if you enjoy eating the dead flesh of a butchered animal—then how humane are you really?

We all need to take a good look at our level of humanity.

Why is nonviolence the wave of the future?

To be future oriented does not simply mean using high-tech or attending conferences on Space colonization or transliving all over the planet. To be futurized above all is to have enlightened values and ethics. People who are truly future oriented are profoundly humanistic. Because the more we advance into the future the more compassionate we grow— the more we value the preciousness of each and every life.

(In my forthcoming book *Countdown to Immortality* I attempt to show that there will come a time in the twenty-first century when even humaneness will not be humanistic enough. There will come a time decades from now when we will evolve beyond humanism.)

The evolution of life has profoundly heightened our appreciation of human rights. This sensitivity to the value of life is obviously uneven within each society and across the planet. There is still much violence everywhere.

But the trend in the world is toward nonviolence.

There is less violence in the world today than at any time in our past. Everywhere violence is declining.

Violence is declining in relations between parents and children— between women and men—teachers and pupils—employers and employees—leaders and citizens—society and the emotionally ill— society and the criminal.

There is also less violence among nations—among religious groups—among races. There is even less violence toward animals.

If at times it appears that violence is increasing in the world it is only because we are now better informed more interinvolved more humane.

"My own belief is that there is less violence today than there was one hundred years ago, but that we have a much better press and communications to report it"—wrote Dr. Karl Menninger in his pioneering book *The Crime of Punishment.*

We are not only better informed—we are also more sensitive to injustice and inhumanity. What a modern society condemns as violent or criminal was at one time socially accepted—the norm.

Here are some examples of changing norms:

• At one time children were routinely subjected to beatings and humiliations. This was considered "good upbringing." Today we angrily condemn this as "child abuse." In fact a common complaint these days is that parents are now too permissive.

• By today's morality most women in traditional societies were victims of rape. Girls fifteen or sixteen years old brought up in sheltered environments were suddenly required to submit sexually to husbands to whom they were "given" often against their own wishes. Forcible marriage is institutionalized rape.

• At one time everyone walked around openly displaying their weapons: daggers—swords—muskets—pistols. Today many countries have banned the ownership of firearms. In countries such as the U.S. some gun control measures have been passed. But no one is allowed to display weapons publicly.

• The farther back we go in history the more brutally we dealt with crime. Ancient laws were mostly based on vengeance. In England as late as the eighteenth century women—and twelve-year-old children—

were hanged for petty theft and pickpocketing. In North America—Europe—Asia—elsewhere people were routinely executed in public squares. Today the trend in the world is toward the complete elimination of the death penalty. All West European countries and many other nations on all continents have already banned capital punishment. More and more people everywhere regard the death penalty as murder—murder committed by the state.

• At one time people routinely hunted animals for food. Today only the most insensitive among us still go hunting and fishing. Thanks to the vigilance and outcry of "animal rights" organizations hunting of some species of whales and seals and some land-based animals has decreased or even stopped. In fact in modern communities if you pull your dog's ears you may be penalized for "cruelty to animals."

• Until the twentieth century the majority of the people of the planet lived in rural areas. Household members routinely slaughtered animals and poultry for their daily meals. In modern societies today people do not see much less take part in the slaughter of animals. They let the butchers do the dirty work for them. Meat is sold packaged or even precooked or frozen. The connection between the packaged meat and the gory cruel manner in which it got to the dinner table is often lost. Nevertheless more and more people—particularly in the U.S. and in Europe—are waking up to the fact that the steak or hamburger or chicken that they put in their mouths is the dead flesh of an innocent animal that had been slaughtered.

In the U.S. there are now around fourteen million vegetarians. True many of these people have stopped eating meat for health reasons. Still many others are vegetarian because they have arrived at the awareness that eating meat is an act of violence.

• The rule of force is also phasing out among nations. For thousands of years—up until early in this century—conquests—invasions—land grabs—annexations—empire building were commonplace all over the world. A strong nation would send over troops or a few gunboats and openly invade a weaker state. Just like that. No declarations of war—no warnings—no explanations. Aggressions evoked no sense of shame or guilt or public outcry—only pride and exultation over the acquisition of new territory and wealth and power.

The wave of decolonization that swept across the planet in the 1950s and the early 1960s undid much of the usurpations of previous centuries. Today there are only a handful of occupied territories in the world.

Conflicts among nations are now mainly ideological and economic. Major powers have difficulty even maintaining "spheres of influence"—let alone conquering weaker states. The age-old drive to invade and colonize has given way to efforts at winning alliances—markets—coproduction ventures. To win special favors major powers often have to send over foodstuffs or high-tech. This is a new phenomenon in relations among nations.

Two quick observations about violence in today's world:

1—Violence in the more advanced societies is mostly committed by the backward and the disadvantaged. A few years ago the U.S. Commission on the Causes and Prevention of Violence reported that "the poor, uneducated individuals with few employment skills are much more likely to commit serious violence than persons higher on the socio-economic ladder . . . Violent crime in the cities [of the U.S.] stems disproportionately from the ghetto slum."

The point here is that as people advance socially and materially they are less impelled to resort to violence.

2—Some of the violence in the world today is sparked by the collision of social classes—religions—races—nationalities coming together as never before. This unprecedented convergence of peoples of the world has helped bring to surface age-old prejudices and grievances while accelerating rising expectations. As I see it this violence is transitional—the beginnings of communication among peoples who previously had had no contact.

To sum up: There is still much violence in the world—but the trend everywhere is toward nonviolence. The norms are changing.

There are evidences of a refining process everywhere.

More and more societies disallow child beatings (child abuse).

More and more societies now have strict laws against wife beating.

More and more societies have done away with the death penalty.

More and more societies have strict laws against the ownership of firearms.

Sweden and all East European nations have banned professional boxing. Other nations are now considering such bans.

Sweden and Finland have banned the sale of war toys. There are persistent outcries against such toys in Western Europe and in the U.S.

Sweden discourages the public showing of violence in films and on television. There are more and more protests in other countries against violence in the media.

"Animal rights" organizations and activities are proliferating—particularly in North America and in Europe.

Peace movements and disarmament efforts have spread to all continents.

Global telecommunication and convergence are helping speed up the spread of new values and ethics.

In a few decades—say around 2020—there will probably be no death penalty anywhere in the world. We will look back aghast that until the final years of the twentieth century some people in so-called advanced societies still supported executions.

Hardly anyone will hunt.

In advanced societies fewer and fewer people will eat meat. Such eating habits will generally be viewed as barbaric.

Boxing will probably be banned everywhere. American football will be rid of all the violent tackling and hitting—which today cause an estimated 60,000 bodily injuries every year.

Violence in our entertainment media will be discouraged—if not altogether disallowed.

If trends of recent decades continue there will be no invasions of countries.

The nuclear arms race will probably long before have phased out.

We will certainly have our share of problems—interpersonal and global and extraglobal. But we will increasingly deal with problems in nonviolent ways.

We will hardly even notice our relatively nonviolent environments. Just as in modern societies today we are hardly aware that we have steadily outgrown violence in more and more areas of our lives.

What I want to stress here is that the more backward we are the more violent. The more we advance the less we are disposed to violence.

Our level of humanity is one of the clearest indicators of our level of individual and collective growth.

How Immortality Oriented Are You?

1–Do you take measures to help extend your life expectancy? For example:

  A–Are your eating habits healthful?   ____Yes   ____No

  B–Do you exercise regularly?   ____Yes   ____No

  C–Do you have enough mental stimulation?   ____Yes   ____No

  D–Do you smoke?   ____Yes   ____No

  E–Do you drink?   ____Heavy   ____Moderate

  F–What is the stress level in your life?   ____High   ____Moderate   ____Low

  G–How is your fun/leisure/work balance?   ____Balanced____Off balance

2–Would you like to live to 150 years and beyond?   ____Yes   ____No

  A–Is such an extended life span realistic?   ____Yes   ____No

3–If you are critically ill should "heroic measures" be undertaken to save you?   ____Yes   ____No

  A–Have you made arrangements to be kept on life-support systems or in suspension if all else fails?   ____Yes   ____No

4–Should we stop "tampering with nature" and allow people to "age gracefully" and "die with dignity"?   ____Yes   ____No

5–Should we suspend efforts to extend normal life span and focus instead on the "quality of life"?   ____Yes   ____No

6–Are you opposed to life-extension efforts on *logistical* grounds? For example:

A–If millions live to be over 100 where will we put everyone? ____Problem ____No problem

B–If the mortality rate continues to drop radically won't that impose heavy burdens on family and society? ____Yes ____No

C–Won't an aging population slow down progress? ____Yes ____No

7–Are you an ageist (age-discriminating)? For example:

A–"I am too old (or too young) for this kind of thing." ____Yes ____No

B–"You are too old (or too young) for me." ____Yes ____No

C–Do you socialize mainly with people of your own age group? ____Yes ____No

8–Are you a biological purist? For example:

A–Do you think that the human body is a marvel of nature? ____Yes ____No

B–Do you like the human body as it is or would you like to see major changes? ____As is ____Major changes

C–Would you want a total prosthetic body if your own body were irreversibly out of commission? ____Yes ____No

Answer sheet: MONITOR 24

1 A ＿＿Yes (2)   ＿＿No
   B ＿＿Yes (2)   ＿＿No
   C ＿＿Yes (2)   ＿＿No
   D ＿＿Yes   ＿＿No (2)
   E ＿＿Heavy   ＿＿Moderate (2)
   F ＿＿High   ＿＿Moderate (1)   ＿＿Low (2)
   G ＿＿Balanced (2)   ＿＿Off balance

2   ＿＿Yes (2)   ＿＿No
   A ＿＿Yes (2)   ＿＿No

3   ＿＿Yes (2)   ＿＿No
   A ＿＿Yes (2)   ＿＿No

4   ＿＿Yes   ＿＿No (2)

5   ＿＿Yes   ＿＿No (2)

6 A ＿＿Problem   ＿＿No problem (2)
   B ＿＿Yes   ＿＿No (2)
   C ＿＿Yes   ＿＿No (2)

7 A ＿＿Yes   ＿＿No (2)
   B ＿＿Yes   ＿＿No (2)
   C ＿＿Yes   ＿＿No (2)

8 A ＿＿Yes   ＿＿No (2)
   B ＿＿As is   ＿＿Major changes (2)
   C ＿＿Yes (2)   ＿＿No

Total: ＿＿＿＿＿＿＿＿

Would you like to live to 150 years and beyond? Is this realistic?

In the mid-1960s I would ask our futurist seminars at the New School for Social Research: "How many people here would like to live for hundreds of years?"

Only a handful of people ever took the question seriously or expressed interest in living far into the future. Most of the people dismissed the question as frivolous.

"This is a joke"—someone would say. "We can never live that long."

"This is science fiction—not possible."

"Such longevity will not be attainable in our lifetime."

"Who wants to live that long anyway?"

In nonfuturist circles the resistances and skepticisms were even stronger.

These days when I ask this same question at conferences most people respond positively.

Recently I again posed the question at a UCLA (Extension) course in long-range planning. The class was comprised of NASA engineers —industry executives and planners—high-tech specialists—physicians —psychologists—motion picture and television personnel—others. Out of a class of around two hundred people only three had resistances!

Immortality is no longer a dream. Immortality is now science—an emerging discipline. It is also developing into Big Business.

If you are around in 2010 you will have an excellent chance to live to the year 2030. If you are around in 2030—regardless of your age —you will be able to live indefinitely into the future.

If people do not foresee immortality ahead it is only because they are not familiar with the dynamics of human progress. Medicine and genetics can help us prolong the human life span by a few decades. To extend life for hundreds of years we will need more radical interventions.

These upcoming procedures go beyond the purview of this book. They have been thoroughly discussed in another book—*Countdown to Immortality*.

What do you do to help extend your life expectancy?

The future-oriented have a romance with the future. They want to be around to enjoy all the magical worlds coming up.

Too many people still die prematurely because of poor living habits. The leading causes of death in North America and in many European countries are: heart disease—cancer—stroke—accidents—chronic lung disease.

These and other major causes of death are brought about largely by self-destructive habits.

Modifications in your lifestyle can help extend life. These changes are within your control.

- Develop healthy eating habits. Do not overeat and do not go on crash diets. Eat plenty of "protective foods" such as vegetables—fruits—whole-grain cereals. As a rule vegetarians are healthier and live longer than meat-eaters.[1]
- Exercise regularly—exercises tailored to your specific needs.
- Continuous mental stimulation keeps the mind vigorous.
- Do not smoke.
- Drink in moderation.
- Use your intelligence to avoid a stressful life. "Most battles are not worth waging."
- Allow for plenty of leisure and fun. Avoid overload and burnout. People who lead frenzied lives burn out early. In our times you *can* live well beyond a hundred years—if you pace yourself. Work only a few hours every day. Take long vacations.

Plan your life as though you were going to live for hundreds of years. Remind yourself of the Big Picture.

What about the terminally ill today?

If you are gravely stricken—that is not the end.

If all efforts to treat you fail you can be placed on life-support systems or in suspension for treatment at a later time.

Transmit *written* instructions to your physicians—relatives—close friends that in case of "terminal" illness or injury you are to be maintained on life-support until a cure is found.

Sign up with a cryonic suspension organization. (There are several in the U.S. and in Europe.) In case all else fails you will be suspended in liquid nitrogen for reanimation at a later date.

The cures for diseases are coming up fast—one after another. If you stay on hold you have a chance to be eventually treated. If you give up you will be gone forever.

Shouldn't we stop "tampering with nature" and allow people to "age gracefully" and to "die with dignity"?

There is no graceful aging. All aging is graceless.
  There is no dignity to dying. Death is the ultimate indignity.
  Let us stop this self-deception.
  In our times the only dignity is in mobilizing intelligently to *overcome* aging and death.

Shouldn't we suspend efforts to extend normal life span and focus instead on the "quality of life"?

The quality of life is directly tied to the duration of life.
  Try suddenly telling a joyful life-oriented person that he or she has only a couple of months to live. See what that will do to the quality of life.
  Most anxieties and depressions come from the awareness—suppressed awareness—of our mortality. Fantasies of heaven and reincarnation are desperate attempts to assuage profound anxieties over death.
  Survival emotions—love—possessiveness—jealousy—rivalry—fear of separation—etc.—can be traced to the basic fear of death. These emotions play havoc with the everyday quality of life.
  The quality of human life will be enormously upgraded once we do away with death.

If we extend life significantly where will we put everyone?

The radical extension of life span assumes advances in *all* areas of life. Life extension is not happening in a vacuum.
  Where will we put everyone?
  Across this planet—across the solar system and beyond. Space is not an issue.

Won't radical longevity impose a heavy burden on relatives and society?

This assumes that people will always grow old and infirm. Already people are aging more slowly than ever. Gerontologists call this new development "youth creep." The seventy-year-old of today is as a rule far more vigorous than a seventy-year-old of thirty years ago.

We have done away with mandatory retirement precisely because there are now millions of healthy vigorous people sixty and seventy and eighty years old.

What about advances in the next thirty years? The next fifty years? We are not standing still.

As I attempt to show in a forthcoming book early in the new century aging and infirmity will cease to be serious problems.

Won't an aging population slow down progress?

It is a myth that as people grow older they automatically become more cautious. Most people grow more daring as they grow older.

"I was never as old as when I was between twenty and thirty"— wrote V. S. Pritchett the noted English writer at the vigorous age of seventy.

Moreover as noted earlier in this tract—accelerating progress makes for a progressive world. Everyone is continually catalyzed to move forward—often without their own awareness.

Are you an ageist?

"Age doesn't matter"—someone once observed prophetically—"unless you are cheese."

"How old would you be if you didn't know how old you are?" asked a wise Satchel Paige who was a major league baseball star in his fifties.

This has never been more true than in our times. In the age of genetics—reconstruction—rejuvenation—replacement of aging parts —age means less and less.

"How old are you?"

"How old am I? What does that mean? My breasts are twelve years old. My right hip is nine years old. My heart valves were installed five years ago. My new face is only two years old.''

Imagine what a monkey wrench this throws into astrological ''readings.''

''What is your sign?''

''My nose is a Gemini. My penile implant is a Taurus. My electronic bladder is a Libra.''

Are you a biological fundamentalist?

In the 1950s the idea of synthetic replacement parts for the body was considered at once farfetched and repulsive. People believed that such interventions would ''turn us into robots.''

Today tens of millions of people all over the world are alive because we are able to replace nonfunctioning body parts with effective substitutes.

If we want to extend each life far into the future we have to make still more radical changes. We cannot live for hundreds of years with these fragile limited bodies.

Those who want to live forever should be prepared to accept profound transformations in *all* areas of life.

How Transhuman Are You?

1– Do you have a high-tech body? In other words does your body comprise any implants—transplants—smart limbs—electronic monitors—etc.?　　＿＿Yes　　　　＿＿No

2– Does your brain contain a pacemaker—electrodes—other peripherals?　　＿＿Yes　　　　＿＿No

3– Have you undergone major body reconstruction? For example: total face rejuvenation or radical body recontouring?　　＿＿Yes　　　　＿＿No

4– Are your body processes such as moods—cycles—body temperature—etc.—continuously telemonitored and regulated?　　＿＿Yes　　　　＿＿No

5– Are you teleconnected to people and services via onbody (portable) telecom?　　＿＿Yes　　　　＿＿No

6– Are you androgynous?　　＿＿Yes　　　　＿＿No

7– Do you contribute to reproduction only through new collaborative asexual methods? For example:
A– Have you ever donated your sex cells for screening and possible fertilization?　　＿＿Yes　　　　＿＿No
B– Have you ever acted as a "surrogate mother"?　　＿＿Yes　　　　＿＿No

8–Are you a product of asexual insemination or inovulation—in vitro fertilization—telegenesis—frozen embryo implant?   ____Yes   ____No

9–Are you postterritorial: free of kinship ties—ethnicity—nationality?   ____Yes   ____No

10–Have you ever been outside this planet on Space missions?   ____Yes   ____No

11–Have you ever died and been resuscitated?   ____Yes   ____No

Answer sheet: MONITOR 25

1	____Yes (1)	____No
2	____Yes (1)	____No
3	____Yes (1)	____No
4	____Yes (1)	____No
5	____Yes (1)	____No
6	____Yes (1)	____No
7 A	____Yes (1)	____No
B	____Yes (1)	____No
8	____Yes (1)	____No
9	____Yes (1)	____No
10	____Yes (1)	____No
11	____Yes (1)	____No

Total: _____

What is a transhuman?

Transhumans (trans) are a new kind of being crystallizing from the monumental breakthroughs of the late twentieth century.

Trans are not necessarily the progressives and Up-Wingers and others defined throughout this tract. In other words trans are not necessarily those whose values and lifestyles and environments are the most modern.

Trans are not simply advanced historical people.

They are the earliest manifestations of new *evolutionary* beings.

Trans are like those earliest hominids who many millions of years ago came down from the trees and began to look around.

Transhumans are not necessarily committed to accelerating the evolution to higher life forms. Many of them are not even aware of their bridging role in evolution.

Trans can no longer be considered specifically human because the premises of biological terrestrial life that have always defined the human no longer fully apply.

Many of the breakthroughs embodied in transhumans are nothing less than the beginnings of the eventual transformation of the human species.

If you score higher than 7 on Monitor 25 you are a rare being—an advanced forerunner of the posthumans who will surely evolve later in the twenty-first century.

CONCLUSION
Aligning and Accelerating
Your Rate of Personal Growth

The principal purpose of this book is to help you monitor your rate of personal growth (RPG) and locate problem areas—areas where you may be falling behind.

Go over the twenty-five question sheets and add up your total points.

A total of 700 points and above: rapid growth.

People who score at this level are the progressives—the fluid—the future-oriented—the Up-Wingers—the visionaries.

Such people show admirable growth. They are often in the forefront of major advances unfolding on our planet.

Some are trailblazers in their fields.

People at this level use their intelligence effectively. Here are the reasons:

They are quick to learn the lessons of the past.

Quick to isolate mistakes and not repeat them.

Quick to accept change and adapt.

Quick to outgrow old habits old values old lifestyles old technology.

Quick to anticipate what is ahead.

Such people are least likely to allow hardened emotions to interfere with high intelligence.

A total of 550–699 points: moderate growth.

People at this level: liberals—moderate conservatives—the moderately fluid—the adapters.

Such people show movement and growth. They are not among the first to accept change or adapt. They have difficulty shifting tracks in some areas of their lives. But sooner or later they make the necessary changes.

People in this category rarely take chances. They play by established rules and values. Not surprisingly many of these moderate-growth people attain what has traditionally been viewed as "success": leadership positions—seniority in rank—high income—celebrity.

A total of 400–549 points: slow growth.

People at this level: the conservatives—the middle-of-the-road—the traditional—the cautious.

These people have difficulty accepting change and growth. They do not adapt well. They are not in flow. They are not fluid.

The small changes they make are generated by the momentum of changes around them.

People who score at this level—and lower—often reassure themselves that there is suddenly magically a fallback to the way things were.

"The women's movement has lost momentum—" they'll say. "Women are returning to their traditional roles."

"The sexual revolution has fizzled out. People are going back to marriage and sexual commitment."

"People are returning to religious values. There is a revival of religion."

"Patriotism is on the rise again."

"The pendulum is swinging back."

People who hold such views do not monitor the world intelligently. They do not understand the dynamics of progress. Their faulty readouts come from wishful thinking. And from fear—the fear of change and growth.

A total of less than 400 points: near-zero growth.

People at this level: traditionalists—fundamentalists—purists—revivalists—ultraconservatives.

Such people hardly show any growth. The world in the backdrop changes and this often lends the impression that they too are changing. But the changes are negligible—only enough to keep afloat.

People at this level are in serious conflict with late twentieth-century realtime. They do not like what they see around them. They long for the past.

Such people do not use their intelligence effectively. Their knowledge base is persistently outdated. They show low-resolution monitoring of the world around—faulty playback and feedback and information-process. The results:

They do not learn from the past. They repeat mistakes and unworkable patterns.

They hold on to anachronistic values and lifestyles and public policies—which they often rationalize as sacred or patriotic or on their way back.

Their intelligence is usually sabotaged by calcified emotions.

They have no sense of the flow of history. No sense of what is ahead. Their perceptions of the world are out of focus. Their gyroscopes perpetually point to the past.

They suffer from massive desynchronization.

Such people often ask: "Why should I change? I do not like the changes going on in the world."

If they can choreograph their lives to minimize contact with the world around them—they may be able to coast in their time zones without serious downfall.

The problems mount when they have to operate in realtime. These people drive horse-drawn carriages on expressways teeming with speeding cars. They cause collisions—injurious to themselves and others (marital problems—frequent painful breakups—loneliness—bitterness—alcoholism—alienation—inability to move to new jobs or new professions).

Improving your rate of growth.

Go over the question sheets and see where you may have fallen behind.

Do you use your intelligence adequately to monitor the world around you? Do you think things through?

Do you manage your emotions intelligently?

Does the quality of your everyday life need improving?

Does your leisure/fun/work ratio need balancing?

Are you behind in your use of new technology?

Are you telefficient—making effective use of new telecom to access information and services?

How far along are you in shifting from a high-stress low-yield industrial-age track to a low-stress high-yield telespheral life?

Do your values need updating? For example does your competitiveness depreciate the quality of your life and your potentials for growth in all areas?

Does your lifestyle need realigning? How aware and open are you to new methods of procreation—new options for shared parenting— new networks of intimacy?

Are you sufficiently fluid in an increasingly fluid world?

Does your appreciation of art and culture need updating?

Does your ideological orientation need adjusting?

Does your level of humanity need refining?

How mobile and telecommunitized are you?

Are your loyalties and commitments keeping up with an ever-expanding global environment?

How involved are you in our new extraterrestrial environment?

Are your attitudes to life and death keeping up with all the gains we are making in the immortality movement?

In the Age of Information how information rich are you? How updated are you on the accelerating pace of advances in all areas of life?

Focus on those areas where you are falling behind and see how you can improve your rate of growth.

Most of us are not trained to think of growth. We have a blurred perception of our capacity to move forward.

The fact is that *there is nothing fixed or final about our rate of growth. The rate can be adjusted and improved* in the same way that we improve our bodies at a health club or type A personalities are helped to modify aggressive competitive behavior to reduce the risk of heart attacks and get more enjoyment out of life.

We are all capable of adjusting our rates of growth.

The accelerating pace of progress in the world is ample evidence of our extraordinary adaptability and dynamism.

A few individuals in the "rapid growth" category may in fact need to slow down in certain areas of their lives if they wish to have greater immediate influence on the world around them.

Some people in the "moderate growth" level may be complacent about their success or affluence and not realize that their real growth is not in keeping with their potentials—that they may be falling behind in some important areas of their lives.

People in the "slow growth" and "near-zero growth" categories may have simply fallen into lazy or sluggish patterns. They can do much to speedup their growth rates. In some cases this may be achieved through a conscious effort at making a shift in attitude or in values or in ideology or technology. Sometimes the problem is more complex.

Uneven rates of growth.

In *modern* communities the majority of the people have traces of different growth rates: rapid—moderate—slow. In other words most of us are resistant to growth in some areas—slow to change in others— and quick to grow and adapt in yet other areas.

Most people are at once cautious and daring—conservative and progressive—outdated and updated—past-oriented and future-oriented.

The rate of growth in each of us is uneven.

In modern communities relatively few people are resistant to growth in all areas of life or readily receptive to advances in all areas.

During the years I have worked in the management of growth I have been struck by the remarkable mosaic of disparate growth rates in each person. Most people cannot be pigeonholed as across-the-board conservative or progressive—sluggish or dynamic. Most people are a mix of orientations.

There are people with distinctly conservative political views who are startlingly progressive in other areas of their lives. They may be fluid in their romances and lifestyles. Flex in their work habits. Quick to incorporate new technology. They may telecommute or commute via helicopter. Some fly their own airplanes. They may be staunch supporters of the Space program and life-prolongation movements. They may be modern fun-loving people who coast a lot and travel all over the world for pleasure.

I have met and worked with such people. Are they conservative or progressive—past-oriented or future-oriented?

Then there are the politically progressive who are startlingly conservative in other areas of their lives. They may be staunchly family oriented. They may be attracted only to old art: opera—theater—ballet—paintings. They may be technological illiterates. They may be disdainful of the Space program and of life-extension efforts. They may have strong industrial-age orientations—they may for example be workaholics and fiercely competitive. They may be drawn to the power plays of politics. They may be cynical about progress.

I have met and worked with many such people. Are they progressive or conservative—past-oriented or future-oriented?

There are people who still support the death penalty and the arms buildup and are hawkish in their foreign policies—yet are remarkably gentle with their children and may even be vegetarian out of compassion for animals.

Many of my friends in the U.S. Space program have daring visions of extraterrestrial exploration and inhabitation yet have conventional Middle American values: god—family—respect for leadership—work ethic—patriotism.

What I am saying is that there are progressives with strong conservative tendencies—and conservatives with strong progressive habits.

How does one account for such polarities—such juxtaposed diversities in each of us? How accurate are labels in our times?

Most people seem to want progress in some areas but not in others. The fact is that this is not realistic. You can't have it both ways.

If you want advances in one area you have to be prepared for profound changes in other areas as well.

Aligning your rates of growth.

The ideal is to be progressive in *all* major areas of life—in our values and lifestyles—our work habits and use of technology—our politics and ideologies—our loyalties and levels of humanity.

Such balanced growth rates do not presume that everyone will grow at the same pace. Growth leads to diversity. To be progressive and future oriented is to open up to a universe of limitless options.

It means moving beyond the redundancy of traditionalism. It means continually jettisoning your obsolescences and moving on.

(It is the traditional person and society that is predictable.)

To be progressive is to be creative and imaginative. It means using intelligence intelligently.

Uneven rates of growth in a person—or a society—make for an uneven life. It means that parts of you are hobbled in worlds of twenty or thirty years ago while other parts of you strive to move forward. Parts of you want to fly and soar—other parts hold you down.

Such internal tugs-of-war do not allow for a free expression of creativity and intelligence. They do not allow you to fulfill your growth potentials.

To fall behind in any of the major areas of your life is like piloting an aircraft on an endless runway—never able to gain enough momentum to liftoff.

By monitoring your rates of growth in different areas of your life you can begin to align them and approximate your potentials.

Accelerating change is the norm.

Accelerating change is the norm. Do not expect the pace to slow down.

Above all do not expect a fallback to the way things were.

The pendulum does not swing back. Society is not a pendulum. We do not know less today than we knew last month last year last decade.

There is no going back to traditional ways—in any area of life.

We cannot go back to traditional families and parenthood and couplings.

We cannot go back to industrial-age economics and technology and powerful leadership systems. We cannot go back to small farms and assembly lines and preelectronic environments.

We cannot go back to nationalism and religious or spiritual values.

We cannot even go back to being *exclusively* terrestrial and human.

We cannot go back to the worlds of ten years ago—let alone the worlds of thirty or fifty years ago.

In the age of rapid change there is no conservative trend—anywhere in the world.

Many decades ago people were also sure that they would go back to extended families and farm life and simple technology and animal transportation.

They were sure that the agrarian life would come back. But the agrarian world never came back. It could not come back.

Today too we cannot go back. We can only go forward. Fastforward.

Over fifty percent of the world's population is under twenty-five.

In the United States around 120 million people are under thirty. Their number is increasing every day.

It is this rising age-group that will dominate events in the coming years.

Who are these young people? What kinds of worlds did they grow up in?

First: These new generations know nothing of the Great Depression—the World Wars—the Cold War—racial segregation—patriarchy—puritanism. All these are ancient history to them. Certainly not a part of their emotional reference.

Second: These young generations were born into and grew up in radically new environments: Gender equality—coed dorms—teenage sex—global travel—decentralized authority at home.

They grew up in environments of personal computers and smart machines—interactive telecommunication—replacement body parts—extended life expectancy—extraterrestrial treks—multiplicity of options—accelerating change.

To new generations all this is the norm. The Real World.

These young people have different conditionings than previous generations. Different values and expectations—different orientations to authority and traditions—faster rates of adaptability to change.

Even conservative youngsters start off life from higher orbits than previous generations.

Today's youngsters cannot be forced back or legislated back to the oldworld of sexism—racism—patriarchy—puritanism—lifelong commitments—work ethic—leadership—religiousness—nationalism—finite time and space.

"The mind once expanded by an idea can never return to its original dimension—" wrote Oliver Wendell Holmes.

Young generations are not simply expanded by new ideas. Their entire wirings have been set by new environments.

Still younger generations are coming on line launched by the worlds of the 1980s the 1990s and the new century.

Many of those over thirty are also on the move as never before—catalyzed and prodded on by a rapidly transforming world. In fact many of those over thirty will grow progressively more daring as they reach fifty and sixty and seventy and eighty . . .

The remarkable thing about us humans is our ability to adapt and grow.

In the last twenty years we have seen profound changes in all areas of life. Great as these advances have been—still greater advances—more spectacular breakthroughs—more magical worlds are right ahead.

AFTERWORD
Moving On

- In our world of rapid progress personal growth is more important than ever.
- Growth in all areas of life can be a continuous process. There is nothing final or fixed about personal growth. If you fall behind you can catch up.
- Growth in each of us is uneven. (This explains the erratic nature of world progress.) We move forward in some areas but fall behind in others. Too many people flatter themselves that they are ''progressive''—conveniently ignoring the fact that they lag in major areas of life. We grow best when we grow in *all* major areas. These disparities can be aligned.

Go through the monitors and assess your growth rates in each of the twenty-five tracks.

Focus on those areas where you may be falling behind. See what needs to be done to improve your rate of progress. The stretching exercises in the next section are intended to help you accelerate your growth rate.

Go through the monitors again in three months. Then again every three months. See what improvements you make in a year—in two years—in three years. . . .

STRETCHING EXERCISES

The following stretching exercises are intended to help in several ways:

—Encourage perspective. We forget exactly where we were and therefore lose track of where we are and where we may be heading.

—Stimulate you to think ahead. Looking ahead does not come easily to people. We are not programed to think ahead. We do not have a reference base for the future. Ask people to tell you about the future and they begin right away to tell you about the past.

—Stimulate new and creative ways of looking at yourself and the world.

These questions are derived from exercises I have offered at workshops and seminars in Future Studies. Have fun with them.

Personal perspectives and visions.

1—List five improvements you see in your personality (values—behavior—etc.) in the last ten years.

2—List five upgrades in the quality of your everyday life in the last ten years.

3—List five ways you think your life has deteriorated in the last ten years.

4—List five areas in which you think you are behind the times.

5—List five areas in which you think you are in flow with the times.

6—List five areas in which you think you are ahead of the times.

7—List five social reforms you resisted a few years ago that are now accepted norms or laws of the land.

8—List five technologies commonplace today that you resisted at first. For example: telephone answering machine.

9—List five social—economic—political—international agendas that you now resist but which will probably be accepted norms in a few years.

10—How do you see yourself ten years from now? List five specific changes.

11—List five things you might routinely do in the course of a day in 2005 that you cannot (or would not) do today.

12—List eight specific improvements you would *like* to see in your personality and in your thinking in the next ten years.

13—List eight specific upgrades you would *like* to see in your everyday life in the next ten years.

14—Pick five first names—other than your own—that you would be happy with or may even prefer over your own.

15—Pick five new last names (surnames) for yourself.

16—Pick five desirable nationalities for yourself. List them in order of preference. If you do not identify with *any one* nation or continent then what do you identify with? List some preferences.

17—Pick five desirable lifestyles—or combination of lifestyles—for yourself. For example: a secure marriage. Or a transglobal life with lovers and friends in many of your favorite watering holes.

18—Pick five cities—towns—resorts—combination of places—other than your current area of residence—where you would like to live.

19—Pick five desirable professions for yourself. Or combination of professions. List them in order of preference.

(What are you doing about any of the above preferences?)

20—If you were absolutely sure that you were going to live to a vigorous 150 years (or more) how would that affect your life? List eight specific changes you would consciously make in your life.

21—List your eight greatest wishes—including wishes that may not be possible to realize at present. For example: the ability to fly around freely with only a small mechanism attached to your body.

22—List eight major improvements—however radical—you would like done in the human body.

(When do you think such improvements will be made? In twenty years? Forty years? Ever?)

23—List your top eight priorities for helping improve conditions in the world.

24—List ten people whose company makes you happy.

25—List ten activities (or things) that make you happy.

(After you have identified the people and the activities that make you happy ask yourself what you do about this.)

World perspectives

26—List five ways you think conditions in the world have improved in the last ten years.

27—List five ways you think conditions in the world have deteriorated in the last ten years.

28—List five anxieties the public had in the 1960s—the 1970s—the 1980s that have so far proven groundless.

29—List five expectations or hopes the public had in the 1960s—the 1970s—the 1980s that have still not materialized.

30—List five social—economic—political advances we take for granted today that would have been considered revolutionary twenty years ago.

31—List five existing conditions on the international scene today that would have been considered revolutionary or unlikely twenty years ago.

32—List five technologies commonplace today—considered futuristic ten years ago.

33—List five successful medical procedures today—considered revolutionary ten years ago.

34—List five professions commonplace twenty years ago—now largely phased out.

35—List eight words or expressions commonplace until the 1960s —now hardly used. For example: he is a good provider. Brinkmanship.

36—List eight words or expressions commonplace today—hardly known or used ten years ago. For example: surrogate mothering. Glasnost.

37—List ten likely headlines in the year 2000.

38—List ten likely headlines in the year 2010.

39—List ten likely headlines in the year 2020.

40—List five professions commonplace today to be largely phased out in twenty years.

41—List five new professions in 2005 hardly known today.

42—List five telecommunication systems considered futuristic today—commonplace in 2005.

43—List five transportation systems considered futuristic today—commonplace in 2005.

44—List five new lifestyles hardly known today—commonplace in 2005.

45—List five major developments in global and extraglobal affairs by 2005.

(List five ways all the above advances—items 41 to 45—may affect the quality of your personal life.)

46—List five events of the 1980s that will be remembered twenty years from now.

47—List five events of the second half of the twentieth century that will be remembered fifty years from now.

48—List eight people of the twentieth century who may be remembered fifty years from now.

49—List five events (including discoveries—setbacks—etc.) of the twentieth century that will be remembered one hundred years from now.

50—Name the single most important event of the twentieth century.

Reference Notes

Monitor 6

1. William R. Greer, "In the 'Lite' Decade, Less Has Become More," *The New York Times,* August 13, 1986.

Monitor 9

1. Dr. Meyer Friedman and Dr. Ray H. Rosenman, *Type A Behavior and Your Heart.* Alfred A. Knopf.

Monitor 12

1. Samuel M. Ehrenhalt, "Work-Force Shifts in '80's," *The New York Times,* August 15, 1986.

Monitor 15

1. " 'Lite' Decade."
2. The U.S. Census Bureau. April 14, 1987.

Monitor 16

1. Bruce N. Ames, testimony before California Senate Committee on Toxics and Public Safety Management, May 1986.
2. Sheila Rule, "Road to Good Water Still Unpaved," *The New York Times,* July 10, 1987.

Monitor 20

1. John Dart, "Christianity Called More Humane Than Ever," *Los Angeles Times,* April 18, 1981.

Monitor 21

1. Marjorie Hyer, "Psychiatry Accused of Ignoring Religion," *Los Angeles Times,* May 24, 1986 (Reprinted from the *Washington Post*).

Monitor 24

1. American Cancer Society Dietary Guidelines, March 1984. Follow-up, September 1987.

   Jane E. Brody, "New Research on the Vegetarian Diets," *The New York Times,* October 12, 1983.

   "10 Tips on Living to 100," The American Longevity Association, Beverly Hills, California, 1988.

Suggested Reading

1. Axelrod, Robert. *The Evolution of Cooperation*. Basic Books.
2. Cerf, Christopher, and Victor Navasky. *The Experts Speak*. Pantheon.
3. Esfandiary, FM. *Telespheres* (the postindustrial world). Fawcett.
4. ———. *Up-Wingers: A Futurist Manifesto*. Fawcett.
5. Feinberg, Gerald, and Robert Shapiro. *Life Beyond Earth*. W. Morrow.
6. Fisher, Roger, and William Ury. *Getting to Yes*. Penguin Books.
7. Fuller, Buckminster. *Critical Path*. St. Martin's Press.
8. Kahn, Carol. *Beyond the Helix: DNA and the Quest for Longevity*. Times Books.
9. Kohn, Alfie. *No Contest: The Case Against Competition*. Houghton Mifflin.
10. McWilliams, Peter. *Personal Electronics*. Prentice-Hall.
11. O'Neill, Gerard. *The High Frontier: Human Colonies in Space*. Bantam.
12. Prehoda, Robert. *Your Next Fifty Years*. Ace Books.
13. Restak, Richard M. *The Brain: The Last Frontier*. Bantam.
14. Rosenfeld, Albert. *Prolongevity II*. Knopf.
15. Rubin, Lillian B. *Just Friends: The Role of Friendship in Our Lives*. Harper & Row.
16. Sagan, Carl. *The Dragons of Eden*. Ballantine Books.
17. Stine, Harry G. *Handbook for Space Colonists*. HR&W
18. Tavris, Carol. *Anger: The Misunderstood Emotion*. Touchstone.
19. Weinstein, Matt, and Joel Goodman. *Playfair: Guide to Noncompetitive Play*. San Luis Obispo: Impact Publishers.
20. White, Frank. *The Overview Effect: Space Exploration and Human Evolution*. Houghton Mifflin.
21. Yankelovich, Daniel. *New Rules*. Bantam.

I welcome feedback to this edition and suggestions for the next.

If you or your organization is stuck in some areas and needs assistance to move ahead more creatively and effectively, contact us at:

UP-WINGERS
P.O. Box 24421
Los Angeles, CA 90024